James Hay

Notes of a Trip from Chicago to Victoria

Vancouver's Island, and Return 1884

James Hay

Notes of a Trip from Chicago to Victoria
Vancouver's Island, and Return 1884

ISBN/EAN: 9783337145200

Printed in Europe, USA, Canada, Australia, Japan

Cover: Foto ©Andreas Hilbeck / pixelio.de

More available books at **www.hansebooks.com**

NOTES OF A TRIP

FROM

CHICAGO TO VICTORIA

VANCOUVER'S ISLAND,

AND RETURN.

1884.

PRINTED FOR PRIVATE CIRCULATION.

CHICAGO:

RAND, McNALLY & CO., PRINTERS AND ENGRAVERS.

1885.

Chicago to Victoria, Vancouver's Island,

AND RETURN.

Thursday, July 24, 1884, we leave Chicago at 1 P. M., via the Chicago & Alton Railroad. We have a drawing-room in a beautiful and convenient buffet sleeping car. We have supper in the superb dining car "Charlton," said to be the largest car ever built. In this spacious and beautiful car, with its large windows, large tables, roomy seats, excellent and attentive waiters, and generous bill of fare, we have all the luxuries and comforts of a first-class hotel. Flowers on all the tables and on other points of vantage add beauty and fragrance to that which was already very beautiful. It is a pretty custom on the dining cars on this road for the waiters to adorn the patrons with button-hole bouquets. On this particular car, these bouquets were larger than on the other dining cars. In reply to an inquiry, a polite waiter laughingly explained that the bouquets were made large to correspond with the size of the car, so that not only the car should be the largest of its kind but the bouquets likewise.

It was one of Illinois' hottest days, sultry to the extreme point of endurance. Corn is the leading product of the country through which our route lay, and the corn crop looked promising. Here and there it had been bent down considerably by heavy showers of rain. Much interest was felt in the corn crop this year, because for the preceding two years corn in Illinois had not come up to the expected prolific yield. A rainstorm came on during the afternoon, and lasted, without much intermission, all night. It did not make it perceptibly cooler, and sleep became almost an impossibility. While, however, it was not what might have been hoped, a temporary comfort to travelers, it luckily did not succeed in doing permanent damage to the corn.

Friday, July 25th. We arrive in Kansas City at 8:25 A. M. The Union Depot, used by all the railroads, eleven in number, centring in this city, is on the flats below the city. These flats are lowlands which spread out toward the Missouri and Kaw rivers and the open country lying west. The Kaw river empties into the Missouri a mile or two above Kansas City. Beyond the junction of these two rivers lies Wyandotte, picturesquely spread over rising ground. Kansas City proper is a city set on a very high hill. It is also a city which has a high opinion of itself. It is the correct thing to think and speak highly of Kansas City as long as you remain in it, and it is safe to do so, and entirely satisfactory to the average citizen. It is simply just, not to seriously modify that opinion on second thoughts, after bidding good-bye to this most progressive of Missouri cities. It has all the dash of Chicago, and has the ambition to believe that it will rival St. Louis in population. It now numbers about 100,000. The flats present a busy scene of elevators, pork-packing and other establishments; passenger depot, freight depots and yards; and the numerous railroad tracks radiating in all directions,—to Mexico, California, Oregon, Manitoba; to the frozen North, the sunny South, the Pacific slope, the Atlantic seaboard and the Gulf of Mexico.

We get rooms at the Centropolis Hotel, and drive round the city. The residence portion is constantly improving, and is very fine. Some of the locations present commanding views of a pleasant land. Fine residences are numerous, evidencing widely diffused wealth and good taste and aspirations after comfort. From an elevated point, in the outskirts of the city, we get extensive views in all directions. We have the Missouri in sight above and below the city; the flats, the Kaw, Wyandotte; the flat, wooded lowlands across the Missouri; Kansas City, on the hills; and the rolling, hilly country stretching back from the city to Westport and beyond,—scenes which leave an ineffaceable impression. On former visits, I availed myself of this advantageous point of view, and I return to it always with pleasure.

Kansas City was once, and that, too, within the memory of young people, Westport Landing, and nothing more. Now Westport is a not very important suburb of Kansas City. In the irony of fate the same result has befallen many other ambitious places in this country. Thus, Monterey, in California, now a fishing place and a bathing and pleasure resort, and nothing more, was once expected to become what San Francisco has become. New Buffalo, Indiana, and Michigan City, Indiana, both on Lake Michigan, each expected to be the great city in the West, which Chicago has become. Time disappoints many expectations. The heat was intense to-day.

Saturday, July 26th. We leave Kansas City at 9:50 A. M., via the

Atchison, Topeka & Santa Fé Railroad. The day is insufferably hot. To Lawrence, and on to Topeka, we run for the most part close to the Kaw river. It is very full, from recent rains. Corn and all crops are looking splendid. Farmers can not get help enough to cut and store their crops, and it is even said that some of them, rather than leave the wheat standing which they are unable to handle, are offering it free to any one who will cut it and take it away. This was probably only a loud way of reporting the prolific harvest; but the assertion was made that it was an actual fact. I accepted it, however, as an exaggerated method of statement adopted by some creature endowed with an Oriental imagination and gift of speech. Such crops have not been reaped in Kansas for six years past. Consequently everybody is exultant, Kansas is "booming," and prices of land are going up. One result will be that these money-making Kansas farmers will devote part of their surplus earnings to a pleasure trip East, to visit their old homesteads from which they emigrated, and to spread among their old friends and neighbors the glad tidings of fruitful Kansas, and, by their glowing reports, influence another influx of immigration.

Nominally, Kansas still continues to be a prohibition State. In reality, however, it is nothing of the kind. Prohibition no more prohibits here than it does in other States, in spite of an ex-Governor of Kansas to the contrary, "who," said one of my informants, an indignant Republican, "was the first Republican candidate for Governor who lost his party the State, and was deservedly 'snowed under' by thousands of adverse voters." As it is the last day of the week, cases of champagne and car-loads of beer are arriving and being unloaded and delivered at all stations. The railway company takes the side of safety, as it usually does in all cases of doubt, and declines to carry this traffic. The express companies, therefore, have a monopoly of it. These illegal consignments arrive, usually, on Saturday and Sunday.

It appears to be the experience that prohibition condenses the drinking custom to fractions of time, forces it to special days, and impels to periodical heavy drinking, instead of leaving the drinker free to spread his drinking thinly over every day, and imperceptibly attain and retain habits of strict moderation. I have known it to happen in British cities in which a Sunday liquor law existed, that the poor man, who would otherwise have been content with a glass in moderation on Sunday, laid in a stock, in self-defense, on Saturday night, which he used before Monday morning, just because he had it handy. Moderate drinkers are thus sometimes made immoderate drinkers by unwise legislation, brought about by popularity-hunters, and well-meaning but weak-minded people who leave human nature out of their count. Such is the perversity of nature that it refuses to be put in prohibition moulds or other inventions of strait-jacket reformers. At Topeka, the capital of Kansas, where we dine, I am told that I can get wagon loads of beer, etc., over the way. A resident of Kansas City interpolates, that Kansas City, which is a Democratic, non-prohibition city in the Democratic State of Missouri, permits no drinking on Sunday, and on that day the curious sight can be witnessed of citizens of Kansas City, Missouri, going over to the prohibition State of Kansas to do their liquor-drinking.

The leader in this prohibition movement appears to be in bad odor outside the clique which follows him ; and but one opinion about him was expressed to me, that he was a mere self-seeking politician aspiring to power and office, who had mistaken his way ; and that, if he thought any other path than prohibition lay open to him to power and pelf and position, he would walk therein. It has already been said that he lost his party the State ; and at a later date he lost the same party his country. He lost the Republican party the presidency of the United States by running on a Prohibition ticket for President, and drawing away just enough votes from the Republican party to defeat the Republican candidate and elect the Democratic one. Angry Republicans roundly declare, that for this he is to have Democratic reward, or, at any rate, that by his candidacy he has advertised himself so extensively that he will be in demand as a lecturer on total abstinence, and gather ducats galore. His candidacy was widely distrusted, the Republican organs opened vials of political wrath upon him, and the organs of all parties exposed relentlessly to view the sores of his social life, and he was burnt in effigy in a few places. His election cry, "Vote as you pray," had the taint of cant in it ; he stood as much chance of being elected to the presidency as he did of being elected to the papacy, and it is only reasonable to suppose that he knew this just as well as everybody else did.

After passing an uncomfortably hot day, we arrived at Newton, Kansas, at 6:20 P. M. Ladies on the train, and who were from Louisiana, said that it was hotter than in Louisiana. They looked forward with apprehension to a hot night in the sleeping car, and envied us our stop over at night at Newton. But it was so hot that night in Newton, that we were hardly disposed to admit that we could have had a more sultry experience in a sleeping car. Our plan, however, was, as much as possible, to stop over at night, and travel in the day time, so as to see all that we could of the country.

Sunday, July 27th. We leave Newton at 7:30 A. M., and begin to-day to renew acquaintance with prairie dog villages. Fine crops

Prairie Dog Town.

continue to come into view, and we look out at intervals on vast herds of cattle and horses. We arrive at Dodge City at 2:40 P. M., and depart from there at 1:45 P. M. This incredible feat was made possible by the change of meridian time taking effect westward at this point. We turn our watches back one hour, and indulge in heterodox explanations of the way in which the Prophet Isaiah of old manipulated the dial of Ahaz. Turning back time is not so much of a miracle in our day as in that of Hezekiah.

At Dodge an immense herd of cattle is fording the Arkansas. The picturesque cow-boy assists in this crossing. We have seen him several times as we have come along. In Dodge we see him ; and we also see his ponies, many in number, tied up to posts in the street, while he irrigates his constitutionally thirsty soul in some drinking saloon. Distance lends enchantment to the view when the cow-boy is the object of vision. He looks not amiss afar off on horseback, distance softening the outline of his figure, and effectually concealing the outlines of his face : near at hand he is not by any means alluring. It does not occur to you that it is desirable to culti-vate his acquaintance, or to think of him as intellectual. If he drops into literature, it is that of yellow covers and unutterable con-tents. His tone is loud ; his language is plain, but not particularly edifying, and usually consists largely of selections at random from Ho y Writ, not in that order, nor of that kind, which is pleasing to ears polite or pious. He rides fast, drinks fast, lives fast, and it sometimes falls to him to die fast. He is doomed to disappear like the buffalo and the Indian. Meantime, red-shirted or red-belted, armed, and mounted on a fleet steed, he is not an unlovely streak of color on the distant horizon. He becomes worse than commonplace, and has a touch of something more dangerous than disagreeable, as he comes closer.

In Dodge recently an ex-United States marshal went gunning for a United States marshal. These two distinguished citizens—one an "active and intelligent" official, and the other an "active and intelligent" ex-official—were looking for each other (which is, I believe, the correct way of expressing it), and opened fire on sighting each other, and one fell. We gazed from the train on the historic spot of this encounter. Verdict of good citizens of Dodge : "Pity that both had not fallen in the fray : Dodge could well have spared both."

The Arkansas river has been alongside for some distance, having been first noticed at Great Bend, so called from the bend in the river. It remains in sight the greater part of the way until Pueblo is reached, where we cross it twice, having previously crossed it twice, once at Granada, and once about twenty miles west of La Junta. At Cimarron, we come upon the scene of a cyclone of last night. The houses here are chiefly of the adobe style of architecture, with varia-tions. They have been unroofed and much damaged, but fortunately are of an order which can easily, rapidly and cheaply be repaired, or entirely reconstructed.

Within the memory of very young men, these vast prairies over which we have passed the last two days were grazing grounds of buffalo, and were dangerous from Indians : now they teem with rich products, and are rapidly becoming populous with a race who make the school-house the biggest and most prominent landmark in their progress west. We arrive at La Junta at 9:40 P. M. Here one line of railroad diverges to New Mexico, Mexico, Arizona and California, and the other continues on to Pueblo and Denver, there to connect with lines to the Pacific coast.

Monday, July 28th. We leave La Junta at 7:40 A. M. There is nothing big about it but its school-house, which is most creditable to it. The abode of learning was large, substantially built, and well located. It faced the railroad station, of which our hotel was a part, and was a pleasant object of contemplation from our windows. Along the street opposite, and on the other side of the railroad track, in the early morning, there straggled along, in an uncertain and anything but straightforward manner, a drunken loafer, who appeared to be making himself unpleasant to the few people who were abroad at that hour. Tacking eccentrically, he propelled himself into a meat market, which is the Western descriptive for butcher's shop. There must have been some sudden unpleasantness; for we speedily saw him thrown out on the sidewalk by the proprietor of the market, who, after performing this feat, returned to his store and his work. The loafer picked himself up and went on his way, meeting two pedestrians, to whom he explained his unpremeditated and lightning exit from the meat market; but they did not appear to sympathize in his view of the case.

Soon, on our journey westward from La Junta, the Spanish Peaks, and Pike's Peak, and the great range of the Rocky Mountains, come in sight. Some idea of this immense range can be attained by considering that its area in the United States is very nearly eleven times that of Great Britain. We run alongside of it and in its foot-hills all the way from Pueblo to Denver. These two cities appear to have remained about stationary in population for the last two years. We gaze on snow-capped mountains, catch glimpses of Colorado Springs, the Garden of the Gods and Monument Park ; and at 1:20 P. M. lunch at the divide, now called Palmer Lake; elevation, 7,237 feet ; distance from Denver, 52 miles.

From this elevated point, the water flows in opposite directions,

Spanish Peaks, from Veta Pass.

Snowy Range.

northward to the Platte, a tributary of the Missouri, and southward
to the Arkansas. It is the point of division on the watershed, and
took its old name from that. A beautiful little lake adorns this
height, and from its midst a fountain plays unceasingly. Its shores
are kept in good order, and spacious pleasure grounds lie all around

A Glimpse of Manitou and Pike's Peak.

it. There are a band-stand and swings and similar accommodations
for fun-loving children. With mountains all around, in a dry and
rarefied and wonderfully curative atmosphere, in charming locations,
we have an hotel for visitors, summer villas, pavilion for shelter and for
dancing, parks, deer; Monument creek, with its cascades; beauties
in pine and sycamore, moss and shrubs and wild flowers. It is a

Sunday pleasure resort for Denver, and on that day special trains are run, which are well patronized.

The most striking natural object we pass between the divide and Denver is Castle Rock, thirty-three miles from Denver. It is a prominent portion of the foot-hills of the Rocky Mountains, and has a most

Monument Park.

castle-like look; but it is gradually lessening in size, great boulders have chipped off and rolled down, more will follow, and an age will come when Castle Rock will be only a memory, or a line in a book. Time conquers all things.

We have passed a few prairie dog villages between Pueblo and
Denver. We arrive in Denver at 3:15 P. M., and at night go to the
Tabor Opera House, one of the show places of Denver, of which its
citizens are justly proud. The exterior is imposing, the interior
spacious and attractive, the seats roomy, and the ventilation excep-
tionally good.

Tuesday, July 29th. We drive to the fine Exhibition Building,
and through the principal streets. Denver has fine private and public buildings,—among them the County Building, the Windsor Hotel,
at which we have our quarters, the Union Depot, and the High
School. It has also thirty-six common schools, large, airy, well built,
lighted and ventilated. Its school buildings are not surpassed, if
equaled, in any other city in the Union. Pure water is much cared
for and sought after. The hotel at which we stay has its own artesian
well, which supplies water perfectly free from all impurity, and clear
as crystal. The American Hotel also has its own artesian well, and
other hotels will doubtless be spurred on by rivalry to similar acqui-
sitions. A splendid site on high ground directly facing the Rocky
Mountains has been set apart for the Capitol buildings and grounds.
What sublime decrees ought to be the result of such an outlook!
With the snow-clad summits of the sublimities looking down and in
upon them, surely legislators will not dare to be mean in mind nor
paltry in performance.

It rained during our drive. It makes as much fuss about a
shower here as a hen does cackling over a newly laid egg; threatens
what it will do long before it settles down to business; shakes the
trees as if it were going to blow them down, whirls the dust in clouds
as if it were a simoom, and does its best to scare everybody and make
everything shiver and shake and quake. It can be seen afar off,
coming on blustering, black, and as bogey looking as it can make
itself. Then it reaches us, and rains for ten minutes, or, perhaps, by
a great effort, half an hour. This is its usual course. It bullies and
blusters, and tries to terrify by putting on a formidable and dismally
foreboding appearance, and ends by a brief and impotent performance. Rain is not much of an element here. Nobody cares for it,
or depends upon it, or expects anything from it. When it threatens
most, it is not even relied upon to lay the dust. It progresses in
power, however, and, if it only perseveres, may yet achieve success.

Irrigation is the thing in Colorado. It produces prolific results.
They raise fine crops by irrigation; and there is no reason why they
should not raise a fine race of men, as the latter irrigate themselves

even more copiously than they irrigate the soil. In the East they go out "to see a man." In Colorado they "irrigate." "Let us irrigate" is the way in which they invite you to practice at the bar.

The Windsor Hotel is palatial in every sense of the word; and in views of it, on its envelopes and letter-heads, it appears with the lofty, snow-clad Rocky Mountains for a background. Nothing can be finer than that point of view; but there is another, which reminds us of nothing so much as of that single step which Thomas Paine and Napoleon the Great and other celebrities have told us divides the sublime from the ridiculous,—on one side, the magnificent snowy range; on the other, hovels. " Ermine and vermin, magnificence and rats."

In one direction we look out from this regal hotel upon the marvelous white-hooded mountains; in another, we look across the street on hovels and shanties, and low, mean, rickety buildings most anti-palatial, and yards of ill aspect and noisome. In front of us is the son of sunny Italy, unclean, uncanny looking, unsavory and altogether unattractive,—not the son of ancient Rome, nor of the Rome of Mazzini and Garibaldi. This unwashed, unshorn foreigner presides over a fruit stall of unsteady understandings, of which it is impossible to suspect good things. These are contrasts inseparable from new cities, which time will amend. Denver can stand contrasts like these, although it can not be said to care for them, and is fast getting rid of them, and is a city to be desired of man even after everything has been said against it which can fairly be said. We have come from Chicago to Kansas City, 489 miles; Kansas City to Newton, 201 miles; Newton to La Junta, 370 miles; La Junta to Denver, 184 miles; a total of 1,244 miles.

Wednesday, July 30th. We leave Denver, altitude 5,200 feet, at 11 A. M., and at 2:40 P. M. arrive at Manitou, eighty miles distant, altitude 6,370 feet. We retrace part of the way we have come seventy-five miles to Colorado Springs, and transfer to a branch line of five miles to Manitou, where we take a drive of about six miles, going first to Williams Cañon. It is marvelous to see how the wind and the rain have scooped out, torn and chipped, mined and undermined, these immense walls of rock. I make an attempt to climb to the " Cave of the Winds," which is near the summit at one side of the cañon; but, after climbing nearly to the top, find it too hot work, and content myself with taking in the various views from the point attained, and make a leisurely descent.

The seductive advertising card of this cave apprises me of what I

Williams Canon.

have missed: "This cave is not equaled by any attraction in the State. Aladdin's lamp never disclosed such wonderful scenery. It is an elfin ramble, and the centre of scenic beauty." Upon which followed details of scenery. Having read the "Thousand Nights and One Night," I distrusted this card and its amazing claims, and clung to my faith in the splendid incredibilities of the magical lamp. Having wandered for miles in the Mammoth Cave of Kentucky, I doubted of more wonderful caves.

After exploring the cañon and picking up specimens which would make the heart of the geologist leap for joy, I rest upon a huge boulder, and pore upon the brook which babbles by, until a shower sends me for shelter to the hut at the foot of the pathway to the cave. While waiting for my companions to return, a youth inquires his way to the cave, and I play amateur guide, and direct him. He sets off at a high rate of speed, and does some fast walking. I put to immediate use my small knowledge of mountain air and of climbing these heights, and hail him with the startling information that he must restrain himself, or he will drop down breathless, and never reach the top, and may even fail to be "interested" in "the subsequent proceedings," including the rapidity with which he may reach the bottom by new and hitherto

Rainbow Falls.

unexplored ways. Being made to understand that he can not climb high and fast in this rarefied air, and that it will take all the breath he has to go slowly and high, he nurses his breath and ascends.

Then we drive up the Ute Pass, another cañon, and a highway to Leadville before railroads abolished it as a highway, and superseded the numerous teams which traversed it. Leadville, from a mining camp, rose to be a great mining city, and needed and was provided with a railway, but not by way of the Ute Pass. We drove as far as Rainbow Falls, the chief glory and attraction of this cañon, and well worth a visit. We scrambled about the rocks at its foot, getting near

and good views ; but, as there was no sun at the time, no rainbows
could be seen.   Afterward we drove on the trail to Pike's Peak as far
as the Iron Ute Spring, and tasted its healing waters in the natural
state, and also as manufactured into lemonade.   Previously we had
visited and tasted the other mineral springs, five in number, two of
them close together, but of widely different qualities.   Carbonate and
sulphate of soda prevail in all these springs, including the Ute, and

Pike's Peak Trail

carbonate of magnesia in five of them.   The waters in some effer-
vesce very freely, and bubble up in unlimited supplies.

Pike's Peak is 14,147 feet above the level of the sea.   Snow lies
on the top all the year round.   The United States Government has
a signal station on the top in connection with the Weather Bureau

in Washington,—Old Probabilities, or more familiarly known to us all as "Old Probs." It is twelve miles by foot and bridle path to the summit, and during the summer parties are made up early every morning, who accomplish the trip there and back on horseback in one day. By looking long and carefully and training the eye to the work, we discern, as specks in the distance, horses and riders threading their way down the mountain. The Pike's Peak railway is being built to the top, which will increase the distance to thirty miles, but will make the trip one of ease and pleasure, and less of labor and fatigue than it is now. This railway will mount two thousand feet higher than the Lima and Oroya railroad in Peru. Its entire length will be a succession of complicated curves and grades, with no piece of straight track more than three hundred feet in length.

Thursday, July 31st. We start early, with a programme made out for all day, and take a carriage drive of over thirty miles to the Garden of the Gods, Glen Eyrie, Colorado Springs, and North and South Cheyenne Cañons. A capacious hamper jammed full of various supplies relieves us of all apprehensions on the score of commissariat until supper time, which is the hour at which we purpose to be back. We enter the Garden of the Gods by the south entrance, instead of by the gateway, as on my first visit, a few years ago. "Balanced Rock," close to the entrance, first attracts the eye. It is about fifty feet high,

Balanced Rock.

thirty feet thick at its greatest breadth, stands on a point of about three feet, and weighs many tons.

The garden is about two miles in length and one in width, and grows only rocks of wondrous form. It would take many days to thoroughly explore it, and see it, as it deserves to be seen, in all its details. Such an exploration would be replete with pleasure and constant surprises. We drive very slowly through it, stopping every

now and again to get a closer and longer view of some marvel, or to
look beyond the garden to the mighty and wondrous range of mountains alongside, stretching away far out of sight.   All kinds of grotesque figures in rock meet the sight,—old man, toad-stools, hooded
figures, seals, frogs, deer's head, Mother Grundy, dog's head, lion,
Tower of Babel, elephant, Cathedral Rock, and many more catalogued
in guide books ; but no guide book nor any description can convey
an adequate idea of this astonishing garden.

Garden of the Gods.

We pass out at the gateway, which is perhaps the crowning
wonder of the place.   It is a veritable gateway, of prodigious size
and imposing altitude and appearance, minus the gate.   As far as we
can see, and one can see far in this clear atmosphere, we keep looking back at these majestic portals to this garden of giant wonders.

Glen Eyrie has a cañon which, in comparison with the great
cañons, may be described as a baby cañon.   If it may be permitted to

speak of a cañon in this way, it has something about it gentler, quieter, more refined, more delicate, more human, and that can be more easily grasped, than the larger cañons. I saw it some years ago, but could not see it to-day. All the ground about the entrance has been preëmpted, and occupied as private property. A gentleman's residence and grounds bar the way to this natural wonder, hide it from view, and make it a mystery,—a suppressed, secluded, imprisoned wonder, instead of an open marvel. It is an outrage to

Garden of the Gods.

permit any one to make private property of scenery like this. As well preëmpt Niagara Falls, or demand toll for a sight of ocean. There is a legend that a shrewd citizen preëmpted the top of Pike's Peak, and that much persuasive power was required to convince him that the United States Government was a "biger man" than he was. He was ultimately compelled practically to assent to the precedence of the claim of the government over that of any citizen.

We were permitted to drive about the beautiful grounds of Glen Eyrie, in part shut in by the Rocky Mountains, and on another side by perpendicular natural walls of great altitude. High up in these walls, 1 noticed the huge nest of an eagle, supposed to be the same nest I saw on a former visit, as it was in the same spot. Some natural columns of rock in these grounds are about one hundred feet high, and at a distance look like monuments erected by man. As we drive from Glen Eyrie to Colorado Springs we get distant views of the Garden of the Gods; and the range of the Rocky Mountains, as far as the eye can reach, comes into full and splendid view.

Colorado Springs is four square miles in area, is five miles from the mountains, and at an altitude of 6,023 feet. It is about fifteen years old, has a population of over 6,000, and is beautiful with trees and flowers and small parks. Through the streets, which are wide, and lined with shade trees, water flows freely, and in unlimited volume, in irrigating ditches. The water supply for irrigating and drinking purposes is said to be practically unlimited, and, coming, as it does, from lofty mountain heights, gives a pressure which makes fire engines superfluous. We drive through a broad street, with two rows of trees in the centre, and a row on each side, and which is intersected by several small parks.

The drive to the Cheyenne cañons was mainly over a road by a pleasant brook, and sheltered by trees. We drove nearly as far as the carriage drive extended in South Cheyenne Cañon, and then took lunch in a wood cabin, with the clear waters of the cañon flowing on both sides of us. It was a hot and tiresome walk to the Seven Falls of the Cheyenne; but the wonders and the beauties of the way, and the culminating sight of the Seven Falls, made us glad that we had not missed a foot of the distance. In a succession of seven falls, the sweet mountain stream makes its descent from the mountain top to the bed of the cañon. At the foot of the lowest fall, the topmost ones are not in sight. I climbed to where I could see the whole series above and below; but this was not half way to the top. I had enough of climbing, and rested and made a leisurely descent, and lay on a boulder at the foot of the lowest fall, and in front of it, listening to its voice and enjoying its coolness, until rejoined by the rest of the company.

Afterward we drove about two miles up North Cheyenne Cañon in wooded ways by a delightful stream, the bed of which is chiefly a series of little falls. The two cañons are a little less than a mile apart. In both, the mountains rise to a great height on either side, and huge and curious shapes of rock arrest attention. The North Cañon was the finest drive, and was more beautiful with trees.

On our return in South Cañon, as we passed the hut at which

we had lunched, it was being taken possession of for the night by a party who were camping out. We saw more than one team, each with a party who had all the requisites for camping out. To sleep in this vagabond, Bohemian way in these wonderful cañons, seemed a new kind of pleasure. After a drive of nearly ten hours, we got back to our hotel at Manitou, ready for supper and bed. The air of Colorado creates an appetite, and weighs the eyelids down. We drink in this fine air; we revel in it; we take in new life from it. Whatever the days may be, the nights are cool; and the air we have breathed, enjoyed and exulted in, and the cool night, shut down our eyelids, and compel refreshing sleep; and, when morning comes, we wake to bounding impulses, feel as if we must skip and bound and play, and are ready and eager for another day of vigorous exercise.

For miles and miles we ride alongside these snow-capped sublimities which form the backbone of the conti-

Section of Cheyenne Falls.

nent. Patiently they stand, and time chips away at them with a patience equal to their own. Change is on them as on all things. Talk of everlasting hills: that is so much nonsense. Time smiles at that, as he persistently and imperceptibly keeps on demolishing them. Age, rain, wind and snow, destructive forces which are only creative forces under another name, chip off boulders, roll them to the plain, grind them to fine dust, and scatter that dust broadcast. The process can be seen as one travels hundreds of miles in and through, over and alongside, this enormous mountain range.

North Cheyenne Canon

What marvels these mountains hold! what tremendous abysses! what awe-inspiring altitudes! what raging torrents! what gleaming waters in pool, rivulet, fall and lake! Now this mountain land is beautiful with trees and flowers; now bleak and barren above the timber line and line of vegetation, and with rents and crevices of unknown depths and dimensions, filled with snow which never appears to decrease in volume. What lessons may be read here by the man who brings to these scenes a receptive, responsive soul! Here the wisest may find more wisdom; the boldest, fear; the gayest, maddest, wildest, some touch of sobriety of thought; the saddest and most sorrow laden, some oblivion, or balm, or patience.

> " If thou art worn and hard beset
> With sorrows that thou wouldst forget;
> If thou wouldst read a lesson that will keep
> Thy heart from fainting and thy soul from sleep,—
> Go to the hills: no tears
> Dim the sweet look that nature wears."

What histories are in these hills! What sermons in these stones! What books in these mountain brooks! He to whom these mountains have not a language, is past all reproof, or help, or inspiration. Under their high influence, life does not look at all a joke, nor a shadow, nor a vain show, but real and earnest. Clouds obscure their summits, or sail over their face, rainstorms rage midway upon them, snowstorms in summer add to the snow which covers their loftiest peaks,—all visible to observers who stand in sunshine below.

An impression appears to prevail abroad, that bigness is the chief characteristic of the sights of this land. The foreigner only hears, or affects to hear, of big rivers, lakes and mountains; and sees, or affects to see, these alone. I do not wish to assist in keeping up the impression that bigness is a peculiarity of our scenery. I read in books and newspapers of other lands, that we have nothing like Lake Geneva, in Switzerland, or " lovely Loch Achray," or other lochs of Scotland, or lakes of England, which, in addition to their other attractions, have become a part of imperishable song, and unforgetable history, and entrancing legend. Yet, we have in the East, Lakes George, Champlain, Memphremagog, Seneca, Geneva and many another; and in the West and in these mountains, countless small lakes of surpassing beauty. It is not thus intended to disavow or belittle those mighty inland oceans, larger in area than European kingdoms ; those great unsalted seas that bear on their broad bosoms the rich argosies of commerce, the priceless products of fertile and sovereign States; but to show that we have also lesser glories in lakes and lakelets of ineffable beauty, of surpassing loveliness, which need not veil their beauties nor pale their boast before the most vaunted of their rivals of other lands.

Friday, August 1st. We leave Manitou at 8:45 A. M., for Salt Lake City, via Denver & Rio Grande Railroad and Colorado Springs and Pueblo, a trip of 666 miles. From Colorado Springs to Salt Lake City we have buffet sleeping cars, in which lunches can be procured at any hour. We cross the Arkansas often. At one point there is a submerged railway track. The Arkansas has fancies, and indulges them. It suddenly changed its course and went by rail, and nobody afterward cared to go the same way, or could have gone if he had so cared. Its waters flow over rails and sleepers where once trains ran. It is inconvenient and expensive; but the river would have its own willful way.

An observation car is put on at Cañon City, that we may sit outside and see all the wonders of the Grand Cañon of the Arkansas, and especially the Royal Gorge.

The Royal Gorge.

There is a blazing hot sun shining fiercely down upon us, and the wind, which is a little unruly, blows right on us smoke and cinders from the engine, and dust from wherever it can find it, and it appears to find plenty of it. We heroically sit it out, however, till we have passed in review the glories and grandeurs of the Grand

Cañon, and have looked on its greatest sight of all,—the Royal Gorge. Here the Arkansas and the railway are compressed to a breadth of only about thirty feet, with perpendicular rocks on each side, 3,000 feet high. The railway for a short distance is suspended over the Arkansas on "an iron bridge built lengthwise with the river, and suspended from steel trusses mortised into the rock walls upon each side." At this point on one side there is a rent in the rock extending from top to bottom.

From Salida, 147 miles from our starting point of this morning, the road runs in one direction to Leadville, and in the other to Salt Lake City. At Manitou the altitude was 6,370 feet ; at Colorado Springs, five miles from Manitou, 6,023 feet ; at Pueblo, forty-five miles from Colorado Springs, 4,668 feet ; at Cañon City, forty-one miles from Pueblo, 5,344 feet ; at Salida, fifty-six miles from Cañon City, 7,050 feet. From Salida we go on ascending, and look up to altitudes to which we must go, and down upon depths from which we have come. We do not go on a level, but go up ; do not go straight forward, but run round and round. We look up, and see high above us, but leading in an opposite direction to our present course, the track by which we shall shortly go. We look down, and see far below, but in an opposite direction to our present course, the path by which we have come. We go many miles circuitously in order to make one mile of straight-forward advance. At one high point, the mountains near by frame a view far below, and which we have left far behind, of a most spacious and beautiful valley, lying in sunlight, and guarded by snow-capped mountains.

Most of the way there are two engines. As we ascend, the engines puff as if their breath were going out, and the cars strain and creak as if the labor of it was physical pain. We look up to amazing altitudes to which we are to ascend, as appears from the outline of the track, which distance reduces to the dimensions of a goat path ; and down, with wonderment, to the depth from which we have come, marked by the thin streak of the railway track far below.

We get within a mile walk of the top of Mount Ouray, the altitude of which is 14,043 feet. In this clear and deceptive atmosphere, it seems only a few minutes' walk to the top. Snow lies on it. Snow lies alongside of us at one place. From lofty points of vantage, we get views of sweet valleys lying in clear sunlight, hemmed in by mountains with snow-clad summits ; far off, but seemingly close at hand ; so near to vision, so far away in actual distance. There are mountains nearer and lower, timber clad ; others with trees

stripped of branches and foliage, bare, and strewed on the ground
like stalks of wheat or corn, or like bare poles left standing. These
are the remains of forest fires. Snow-sheds become common sights.
We pass through many of them before attaining Marshall Pass, at
an altitude of 10,760 feet. From this divide the waters flow in one
direction to the Pacific Ocean, and in the other to the Gulf of Mexico.
There are only ten minutes to take in the view. We are above
the timber line. Vegetation exists in lower regions. We look down
on lofty mountains and lovely valleys,—in every direction mountains
and valleys, both at an elevation of thousands of feet, and both
beneath us. There are four thin strips of terrace below, which are
the lines of track by which we have ascended, and we are to descend
on the other side on similar lines. Flower dealers assail us ; but we
waste not a precious minute of the ten at our disposal, and brush
aside all smaller things, and adhere steadily to sight-seeing.

The ten minutes do not seem as long as ten seconds. We seem
to have had just a glimpse of this wonderland when summoned to
resume our seats and our journey and commence the descent.
Curves and altitudes affect mercurial, excitable people. Two lively
ladies, who have been keeping up a constant excitement, and gener-
ally bobbing around and making things lively, and having solid
chunks of fun, are overcome, and lie kicking and screaming in the
car, when we return to it after our ten minutes' sight-seeing is over.
These ladies were seriously affected, and were made worse by a
crowd of amateur nurses of both sexes, each of whom had separate
opinions and different remedies, mostly absurd and hurtful. A
doctor was discovered at last, who aided in the recovery of the worst
case, and the other recovered without a doctor. Quiet people usually escape these painful faints.

We are alongside the Gunnison river, and night and the Black
Cañon are approaching. I catch glimpses of cañon and river as I lie
in my berth. We cross and re-cross the river. The stream runs
fast, and looks dark ; and the lofty walls of the cañon, two or three
thousand feet high, impress me with the idea that they could make a
night of their own if night were not. Gradually I get too tired for
sight-seeing, and give it up for the day, and try to sleep. Think of
sleeping in this magnificent cañon ; but the mountain air insists
upon sleep. Thus I miss countless wonders, among them the red-
hued Currecanti Needle, described as an abrupt and isolated pinnacle
which has all the grace and symmetry of a Cleopatra obelisk ; but,
judging from a Cleopatra Needle which I have seen, and pictures of

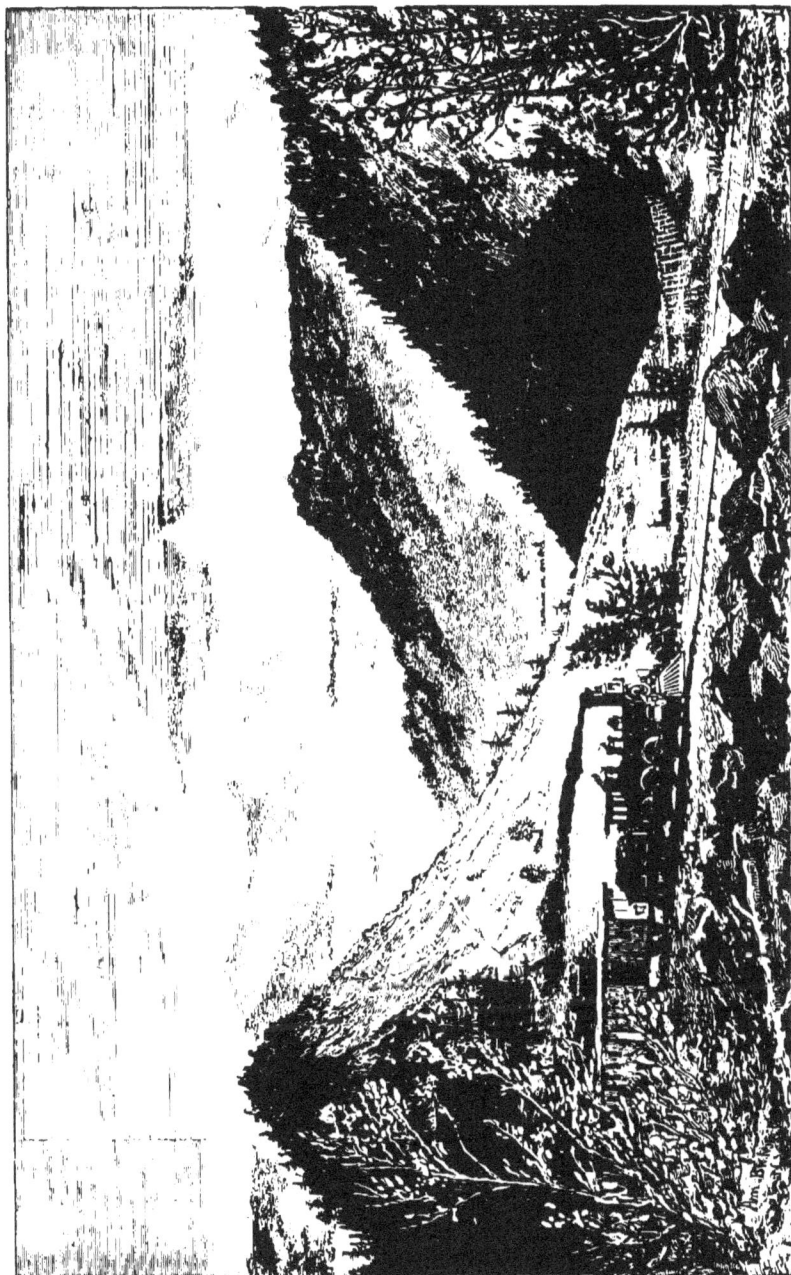

Marshall Pass—Eastern Slope

Marshall Pass — Western Slope.

Approach to the Black Canon.

Black Canon of the Gunnison.

the Currecanti Needle, the needle of the Black Cañon differs from the needle of Egypt, as nature from art.

Next morning, Saturday, August 2d, as we whirl round curves, washing becomes a fine art. Now I hold on to the washstand with one hand, now with both hands. I brace myself against the car, I bump against the water cooler. Washing on the stormy Atlantic, washing on the crookedest road I have ever yet been on, is nothing to this. Crossing the Alleghanies on roads famous for curves and bends, of horseshoe and other varieties, is nowhere in comparison. "Any fool can build a straight road," said a Pennsylvania expert ; "but it takes an engineer to build a crooked one." The engineer of a crooked turn must have expended all his genius on these curves ; nothing more in the way of curvature on the spine of this continent can be imagined or endured.

We come upon washouts, and see where the road would have lain if the mountain torrents had not preëmpted it without law or leave, and in bold defiance of vested rights and the Constitution of the United States. The river holds its way over the old railway track, and we meekly pass by on a new one, which in the future the raging waters, in some mad, whimsical fit, may elect to occupy. Then the railway can again go up higher. Excelsior is a good motto for railway companies in this land of untamed streams and lofty hills. We pass over 100 miles of what has been described as billowy desert, and the surface has a distant resemblance to the billows of ocean ; but even this scenery is shut in by mountain ranges which take it completely out of the realm of the commonplace.

Six hundred and twenty-four miles from Denver we enter Castle Gate. This entrance, or gateway, to Price River Cañon, has two huge red pillars, one 500, and the other 550, feet high. We are now in the Wahsatch range, and are constantly in sight of huge and curious forms of rocks bearing resemblances to man and his works which are common to all cañons which I have seen. We attain the summit of the Wahsatch Mountains, and, passing down Soldier Cañon, the red narrows, and the beautiful and alluring Spanish Fork Cañon, emerge into Utah valley, bounded by mountains on every side.

The first outlying Mormon settlements have small, hut-like habitations, in which it is impossible to imagine comfort of any but the lowest order ; they do not appear to be more than kennels in which to sleep. All this changes rapidly, however, and habitable

3

Currecanti Needle, Black Canon.

and attractive buildings begin to appear. The fields everywhere
give evidence of thrift and industry. The Mormons and the Chinese
seem to have the capacity to get the most out of the soil. Water is
utilized all over the valley for purposes of irrigation. Where man
is his own providence in the use of water on fields, the results look
tropical and profuse.

Castle Gate.

At Springville, a flourishing place, 684 miles from Denver, I
notice a prominent store with this legend thereon, "Springville Co-
op," and find that it is a Mormon co-operative store. There are
no real co-operative stores here, nor elsewhere in Utah, on the English plan. They are simply firms with a numerous partnership.
The members inherit all the spoils. The customers, who are not

members, do not share in the profits on the same plan, nor to the same extent, as in England.

At Provo, we are 689 miles from Denver, and children swarm on the platform with fruit to sell at bankrupt rates. It is offered at an alarming sacrifice when the moment arrives for the train to move. The fine, fresh waters of Utah Lake are in sight. The valley is a scene of beauty, shut in by the snow-capped hills. It is watered by the clear waters of numerous mountain streams natural

In Spanish Fork Canon.

and artificial. The farms look like large gardens; grapes and fruits of all kinds abound. The pretty white houses peep out from amid forest trees or rich orchards of liberal area. The river Jordan flows from Utah Lake into Salt Lake; and beyond Provo, we run alongside of it, and keep near it, until we reach Salt Lake City, crossing it when coming in sight of the city, which, in the distance, seems like a beautiful forest, with houses here and there peeping out. It gradually ascends from the valley, and climbs the lower heights of the mountain range. It is more of a forest city than any which I

Salt Lake City.

have seen; and, in itself and its location on the side of the hills, it would be called beautiful, anywhere. We can see from the train the Tabernacle, the Assembly Hall, the unfinished Temple and the higher buildings.

From the city, the whole Salt Lake valley is in sight, and much of Salt Lake with its mountain islands. The valley is Utah valley -intensified. It is thoroughly irrigated and cultivated, and almost, if not completely, occupied by settlers. Wheat fields, hay fields, market gardens, cattle ranges, take up the available space. The climate is delightful. It is a land of sunshine and loveliness, where health and plenty cheer the industrious tiller of the soil. It has not been inaptly named "the Eden of the West."

The Jordan is a dirty stream, and inspires me with no desire to be baptized in it. Wholly or in part, the Jordan, and streams of loftier source and clearer strain, are taken out of their original course and diverted through the city. Water flows next the sidewalks in every street, in some of which it is clear and rapid and always in considerable volume, and in many places, especially in the best residence streets, looks as if it were a natural stream flowing in its own bed. The saints do not much practice watering streets, and the dust is simply inconceivable. Why people so sensible in many other respects should endure such a permanent nuisance and abomination as this dust, is a mystery of faith which I fail to penetrate.

I pass the Amelia Palace, large and imposing, at one time the residence of the favorite wife of Brigham Young, and now the residence of the present chief of the Mormon church, President Taylor. On the opposite side of the street are the Bee-Hive and the Lion House, once residences of Brigham Young. The Lion House now appears to be used as the principal business office of the church. The Bee-Hive is surmounted by an imitation of a bee-hive; and lions, in stone, lie on each side above the entrance to the Lion House.

In continuation of these, on the same street, and on the same side of the street, and in the same block, are the offices of the *Deseret News*, the official organ of the church, and the most ably conducted paper in the Territory. Next to these, and continued on a cross street opposite the Temple, are the tithing houses, where the saints pay their tithes in cash or kind. The unfinished temple is surrounded by a high wall, and there was no admittance at the hour at which I passed it. "Commenced April 6th, 1853," is inscribed on it.

On one side of a tall, long and well-built brick building of spacious breadth, I read "Z. C. M. I," which, being interpreted,

meaneth "Zion Co-operative Mercantile Institution." It is more
familiarly called by saints and sinners the "Co-op." This legend
adorns its front, "Holiness to the Lord." It does business to the
extent of millions of dollars annually. It is not co-operative in the
English sense of that word, but is a partnership concern, two or three
rich partners holding a controlling interest, and the balance of the
stock being scattered among a large number of small holders. It
has a reputation for keeping on sale good articles, and competes for
business against regular merchants on the regular plan of competi-
tion, under the usual conditions, and with the usual organization and
methods of any ordinary business house.

At one time this institution had a practical monopoly ; but the
gentile from without and schism from within the church undermined
its power. The Walker Brothers, four in number, descendants of a
Mormon, and themselves Mormons, defied and denied the power of
Brigham Young. The issue was on tithes. The prophet thought
that they paid too little, and demanded more ; but they refused to
pay anything, and took the ground that the office of the prophet and
the church was spiritual, not temporal; that the church should not
command in commerce and politics ; and that in civil government
the United States was supreme.

In despite of Mormon influence, the Walkers built up an oppo-
sition trade to the "great Co-op," and have become wealthy and
influential, among other holdings owning the Walker House, the best
hotel in the city; and I was told that they were owners of the
Walker Opera House; but have since seen it stated in print that this
is owned by the McKenzie Reform Club, a gentile organization. In
the battle between the Walkers and the church, Mormons were
forbidden to trade at the store owned by the former, and thereupon
these lines became popular :—

> " Mother, may I go out to shop ?
> O yes, my darling daughter ;
> But be sure to go to the great Co-op,
> And don't go near the Walker."

I ascend to the top of the Walker House, and get a splendid view
of the city. It has long overpassed the limits which its original
founders evidently foresaw for it, if I may infer so much from its
having extended beyond the cemetery which lies higher up on the
mountain slope. Much farther away still, and in the same direction,
lie the United States fort and barracks. The city has kept strag-

Mormon Temple, Tabernacle and Assembly Hall.

gling out toward the fort, and the two are nearer neighbors now than when first they made what promised not to be a pleasant acquaintance. It is claimed that the city streets are twice as wide and the blocks twice as long as in other cities, a claim which any one who · walks them will not feel disposed to contest. These streets are lined with shade trees, and the residence portion is made beautiful with trees, lawns and flowers, and clear, babbling brooks.

There are two opera houses, one of Mormon origin and control ; the other owned by Mormon skeptics, who, as already explained, held the inadmissible and heterodox tenet that the church had no right of control in temporal affairs, but only in spiritual ones. Mormons will not go to the heterodox opera house : gentiles will go to either. Consequently, to insure the presence of both saints and sinners, a shrewd manager, having ducats in view, engages the Mormon opera house. "Mascotte," by the same company that I had seen playing it in the splendid Tabor Opera House, in Denver, was being played here. Wishing to see a Mormon play-house, I accepted a courteous invitation, and was assigned a stage box from which I could have a good view of the house, a most substantial one, like all Mormon public works. It is 80 by 174 feet, with a seating capacity of 1,700.

Sunday, August 3d. I was urged to make an excursion to Salt Lake, and bathe in its waters, and told wonders about the invigorating results of such a trip and bath ; but I preferred to go to the Tabernacle. This building stands in what is known as the Temple block, in which also stand the Assembly Hall and the unfinished Temple. It is elliptical, and roofed with a dome of the same form. The latter has been aptly described as resembling an upturned boat. The Tabernacle is 150 feet wide, 250 feet long, and 90 feet high. The organ was pealing forth solemn music as we entered. We took seats two or three rows from the front of the gallery, at the end facing the organ, orchestra and ministering saints at the other end. The organ is, I believe, the largest and finest on the continent save one ; and the well-trained choir, two hundred in number, is said to be the best west of New York.

The leader appeared to go about his duties in a business-like way, as if he were wielding his baton at a festival or a grand opera. There are twenty very large entrances, fourteen for the ground floor, and six for the gallery. The gallery goes all round, leaving only space at one end for the organ and orchestra. In front of the organ sits the choir, ladies on one side facing gentlemen on the other side. In the centre, where the auditorium ends on the ground floor, stands the sacrament table, a long table with marble top. Behind it there is a bench of the same length, with seats for about twenty officiating bishops. Behind this, and of the same length, rise three crimson-covered rows with crescent-shaped stand for Bible and hymn book in the centre of each row. These seats are for the highest dignitaries of the church, the president, councilors, presidents of seventies, bishops, etc. On each side of the first of these rows, reposes an iron lion, painted to resemble marble. Still farther away, on each side, repose duplicates of these.

Behind the dignitaries, and higher up, is the choir, and farther back still, against the wall, the huge organ. Some of the occupants of the crimson-covered rows were dressed in black, others wore ordinary business suits of light colors. The seats for the audience, sufficient to accommodate 12,000, were plain wooden ones, with wooden backs not too high. A sketch of a bee-hive adorned the wall behind us. With this exception, the walls were bare. The roof had two skylights, and was festooned with evergreens, and with flowers made of paper. The congregation, in point of intelligence and appearance, seemed to be the average congregation usually to be met with in churches of any denomination, except that it was not so showily and gaudily dressed. Fans fluttered as they do in the hot season in all churches and theatres.

The service was a funeral one, in memory of " two deceased servants of God, Bishop Leonard W. Hardy and President W. W. Taylor ; " * the latter one of the presidents of seventies, and son of the President of the church, John Taylor. Bishop Hardy had died in harness, full of years and honors, at the ripe age of seventy-eight years and seven months. He was one of two selected to go with President Wilford Woodruff, when, on the death of the Prophet Smith, and his brother Hyrum, he was appointed by the Council of the Apostles to preside over the church in England. President William Taylor was a young man of about thirty, who had made a reputation for himself as an active and able worker in the church, and a member of the municipal government.

The Mayor and City Council of Salt Lake City attended the services in a body, and accompanied the remains of their respected co-laborer to their last resting place. The bodies had lain on view from 8 A. M. till 10 A. M., and when we entered at the latter hour, the last of the crowds were passing in front of the sacrament

* *Deseret Evening News*, Monday, August 4, 1884.

table, viewing the bodies, which lay there in caskets covered with flowers.

The organ ceased, and at 10:10 A. M., President George Q. Cannon, who conducted the services, gave out the hymn—

"God moves in a mysterious way,"

which was sung by the choir. President Joseph E. Taylor prayed, and the choir sang—

"Nearer, my God, to thee."

Then followed eulogies by President Wilford Woodruff, Bishop Robert T. Burton, President Jacob Gates, President A. M. Cannon, President Joseph F. Smith, and President George Q. Cannon. Then, in a quiet and subdued tone, the head of the church, President John Taylor, closed with a few sentences of consolation and care for the living. The choir sang—

"In the sweet by and by."

The congregation stood up, and President H. S. Eldredge pronounced the benediction; and the services, which had lasted over two hours, were ended.

President George Q. Cannon announced the speakers, as I understood, without previous notice to them. As each was called, he stepped to the pulpit stand, in the centre of the row in which he sat, and spoke from thence. Each excused himself as being unprepared, and as not having expected to be called upon, and said that he would only make a few remarks; and each ended with "for Jesus' sake Amen,"—the last words uttered swiftly as the speaker retired to his seat, and not unlike a tired child ending its prayer.

The impromptu speaking lacked fire, force, enthusiasm and literary finish. No burst of eloquence enlivened the dead level of the talk. There was not even volubility at all times; but there was sameness and slowness, and, with nearly all, hesitations and long, painful pauses, as if the speaker might stick unexpectedly at any moment. The speeches were not grammatical, nor reasoned, nor pathetic: they were the speeches of plain men speaking, in plain, simple words, to plain men. Perhaps there was restraint in them. They were practical, and had a personal interest which held attention. They dwelt on the gain to the departed, which ought to be matter of rejoicing to the bereaved, rather than a cause for selfish grief. The departed had escaped from the evils of this life, and were beyond the persecutions of the wicked and the power of death, and Satan, and sin, and were safe in a land brighter than day. The speaking was a kind of jubilation on these topics, which were insisted upon, and were undoubtedly believed, and, to a reasonable extent, exemplified. It was enforced, too, that death was sweet to the believer, and bitter to the unbeliever; death was held to have no power over the believer.

There was very little in the services to distinguish them from those of any orthodox Christian church, and a slightly inattentive listener of such a church might have failed to discover that he had wandered from his own fold. I regret that I did not hear President Taylor at greater length. He is said to be an able speaker, which I can readily believe. President George Q. Cannon, too, has a reputation which makes it unfair to judge him by one speech delivered under limited conditions. The same reasons should qualify criticism on all these speeches. Mormonism, I am advised, has able speakers and writers. Personally, I am unable to testify as to the speaking; but as to the writing, at least in the daily press, it is undeniable that the *Deseret Evening News*, the organ of the church, is edited with consummate ability.

At the conclusion of the funeral services, the congregation were directed to keep in their seats till the funeral procession had filed out ; and the doors were shut to enforce this order. When the vast audience, numbering about 7,000, was finally allowed to depart, the perfect arrangements for egress enabled the great building to be emptied with the utmost ease and rapidity, and without crowding and hustling. Those on the ground floor, for the most part, moved out in a line as they had sat.

The acoustic properties are perfect. During the services, people walked out and in and about, babies wailed in all directions, restless little ones roamed about at their own sweet will, no one making them afraid, an uneasy young man behind me kept clawing and kicking at the bench upon which I was seated ; and yet, though almost the entire length of the house from the speakers, I heard them fairly well, scarcely losing a word. On the ground floor a lady fainted, and was carried out at a side door, 'without the episode stopping the speaker, or preventing the audience from hearing him.

It was unbearably hot outside ; but the ventilation was good, the doors were open, and, although little air was stirring, it was utilized, and the church was cool. Huge barrels of ice water stood on the ground floor on each side of the church, at the end near the official stands ; and little folks and big folks handed it round when needed, or thirsty saints and sinners walked up and refreshed themselves " when so dispoged."

Nowhere have I seen such common sense in building a church, or in conducting a service. For spaciousness, coolness, comfort, ease in hearing, and convenience of exit in case of alarm, it surpasses all public buildings I have seen or of which I have heard. Happy little Mormons were not made to sit still when their little souls were weary for change. They walked about and changed their seats at will. The sweet humanity to children thus exhibited was new to me in churches. I thought of the weary hours of church service in which I had to sit rigid and bolt upright in my childhood days, and regretted that this touch of Mormon humanity had not then been infused into Christian orthodoxy.

The Tabernacle is strongly built to last, like the Temple, but is not as fine nor as imposing as the Temple, which is built of granite, as if to resist an attack, and stand defiantly forever in spite of man and time and the elements. It is 117 feet wide, 186 feet long, and 200 feet high, with walls sixteen feet thick at its base, and nine feet nine inches thick above the surface. Moons and stars are carved on its exterior, and there is still similar work to be done. It is far from completion. It is not to be used as a place of worship, but is to take the place of the present Endowment House, in which the secret services of the church are held,—services which, so far as we have any light respecting them, appear to resemble the methods and ceremonies of the leading secret societies, with variations of detail and of ritual.

The Temple is built as, of old, temples were builded to God,— no marble front for show, and the less conspicuous parts of the building of poorer material and meaner detail, as if God could be swindled with a front view. The Mormon Temple is good all through and everywhere ; there is no slop work ; the same material and the same careful finish and thorough workmanship exist uniformly in every part : it is just as good in the rear as in the front, in some out-of-the-way corner as in any part most prominent and most exposed to public view. It is a piece of genuine, honest work ; it is real, and there is no pretense about it. The builders evidently believed in God, and that he is not a God of shams and pretense, which but few builders of churches in modern days appear to do. Nearly all these modern builders palm off on heaven fine fronts, and mean details elsewhere, as if heaven could be taken in with appearances and mere outside looks. The Assembly Hall, a granite building of fine proportions, and the smallest of the three buildings in the Temple block, is for religious and other meetings, the same as those held in the Tabernacle.

We drove all over the city, past places already named, the tithing houses, through the Eagle Gate entrance to Brigham Young's property, to heights from whence fine views of the city could be obtained, through most attractive residence streets, past comfortable-looking and elegant homes of Mormons. Water flows plenteously in every street; yet dust covers everybody and everything.

At one beautiful Mormon home we stopped. The owner and his wife were in the front. Our driver called out to him that I wished to see his hawthorn trees, which stood at different points in his grounds, and he came forward and courteously invited me in. I apologized for intruding upon him, and explained that I was an Englishman resident in this country the largest half of my life, and wished to show my daughter, who accompanied me, the hawthorn of the hedges of her father's native land.

" I am English, too," he said. " What part of England are you from?"

I answered: " Northumberland; but I have not seen it for twenty-seven years."

He added: " I am from Yorkshire, and my wife is from London."

The Hawthorn was not the wild Hawthorn of the "loanins" of my native county, but that with the double flower. He had imported it from England. It served me for a text on which to expatiate to the " Young America " by my side on the glory and the freshness of English May, and I did not omit to glance incidentally at primrose dells, just to show that after all there are some things in the mother country. He made me test his lawn, so soft, so velvety, it seemed almost a sin to use it. I never trod on lawn so perfect, so mossy soft and yielding and elastic. He said that he played bowls on it.

" You can not get the deep green of England," I said, " although you come very near it."

He assented regretfully.

The place was loveliness itself, with trailing vines, creepers, flowers, peerless lawn and beautiful trees. Two lines of creepers, forming two sides of a triangle, stretched from the porch to the street, Chinese pattern wise, but many times lovelier in colors than anything made by hand or machinery. His wife smiled when I said:
" It is so beautiful, it must be a temptation to sin, and passers-by

must break the commandment which saith 'Thou shalt not covet.'"
It was an incomparably lovely little spot. He showed me enormous
strawberries, such as I had never seen before. Many if not all of
these Mormons were poor in their native land. They are rich here,
or comfortably well off beyond any day dream they could reasonably
have dreamed in their early, ante-Mormon days.

We drove past the cemetery, and on to Camp Douglas, past the
residence of the commandant, past semicircular rows of ten double
houses, making twenty residences of officers, with lawn in front. The
soldiers' quarters were solid and comfortable, the finest camp I have
seen for comfort and for commanding view ; finer than Fort Snelling,
I think. It has the mountains for a background, and looks over the
city, the lake and the whole valley. Uncle Sam seems to have cared
for these troops, and especially for their officers. Beyond this camp,
and easily in sight, lies the cañon by which the Mormons entered
Utah. We did not wait to hear the band which plays at 8: 30 P. M.,
but drove back to the city, meeting on our way carriages going fast
to the camp to be in time for the Sunday band concert. The moon
was obscured behind clouds, the curtains of night were drawn down
very fast, the mountains became dim away in the distance, and the
valley disappeared. A view from these heights, of the valley bathed
in moonlight, which we had promised ourselves, was denied us.

On July 24th, 1847, the pioneer Mormons, 143 in number, entered
Salt Lake valley. The population now exceeds 150,000, of whom
over 135,000 are Mormons. Over 200,000 acres of land are in cultivation, and $300,000 per annum are expended in irrigation. Salt
Lake City has a population of about 30,000, and covers nine square
miles. It is 4,261 feet above sea level.

Monday, August 4th. I had interviews with Bishop John Sharp,
President George Q. Cannon and President John Taylor. Bishop
John Sharp is Vice-President and General Superintendent of the Utah
Central Railway, and a Director of the Union Pacific Railway. I
found him at the general offices of the Utah Central Railway. The
busy and intelligent officials of these offices are all Mormons. The
Bishop is a "canny Scot," with plenty of shrewdness, ability and
business capacity; affable, accessible and pleasant to meet, as all
these church dignitaries appear to be. He told a good story with
quiet and striking effect. From Bishop Sharp we went to the Lion
House, to see President John Taylor.

While waiting till President Taylor was disengaged,—if he can
ever be said to be disengaged ; as, from what we saw, the outer

office and his reception-room seem to be pretty full of visitors all the time,—President George Q. Cannon came out, and engaged us in conversation. He talked pleasingly, and, in a quiet, gentlemanly, unobtrusive way, almost without appearing to do it, imparted a fund of information about interesting points in Mormon history.

As the advance body of Mormons came through the cañon into Utah, Brigham Young, suffering from mountain fever, lay on a bed which had been improvised for him in a carriage. He directed the driver to turn the carriage across the road to enable him to see the valley, which he at once announced to be their destination. He located the city at once, and, the moment he could rise from his bed, planned the whole city, and determined the site of Tabernacle, Temple, Endowment House, Tithing House, etc. The Tabernacle was built on his plan, and the Temple is being built on his plan. When what he did, and the success of his doings, and the rapidity with which he thought and planned and executed his plans are considered, it is easy to see how his followers could believe in his being inspired. He appears a leader abler than Moses, and having greater difficulties with which to contend. Moses got away from Pharoah and the Egyptians, superstitious and easily befogged, and not very wide-awake ; but Brigham Young got away from and "got away with" this great Yankee people, "the smartest nation in all creation." He plunged into what was then practically the unexplored desert, and dared the dangers of desert, mountains and hostile Indians,—a hostile nation behind him, hostile savages and unknown dangers and privations before and on all sides of him, his destination undetermined, in an unknown, unexplored land. The story was told of Fremont on his trip across the continent which gave him the title of Pathfinder, mistaking Salt Lake and Utah Lake for one sheet of water, and reporting the lake as being salty at one end, and fresh at the other.

Speaking of the freedom permitted in church to children, President George Q. Cannon said : " We like children, we are very easy with them. Brigham Young did not believe, with Solomon, in birching children, and his example and influence led to great freedom being permitted to them."

President George Q. Cannon and President Joseph F. Smith, the latter a nephew of the prophet Joseph Smith, are respectively first and second councilors of " John Taylor, President of the Church of Jesus Christ of Latter Day Saints in All the World." President George Q. Cannon was formerly delegate from Utah in the United States Congress, and would have been delegate still if Mormon votes had counted; but the Mormons have been disfranchised in this country, as Mr. Bradlaugh's constituents have been disfranchised in England. President Cannon gets nearly all the votes; but he is not allowed to take his seat, because he is a polygamist.

President John Taylor received us very kindly. Three seats stand on a small dais, the centre seat a little higher and a trifle better than the other two. The centre seat is for the President, and the other two for his two councilors. I saw a room full of people evidently waiting to see the President, and I hesitated to occupy his time ; but he did not seem disposed to send us away with a merely formal introduction, and, at his request, I speedily found myself seated alongside of him on the dais. " We are cosmopolitan," he said, " and see many who come, and are glad to see them." I do not report all he said, as I might do him injustice by not giving his exact language, and his charming confidence and kindness deserve fair play. He is of English birth and descent, and came to this country when very young. There appears to have been some prophecy, or something akin to it, that the church would pass under the leadership of the English, which prediction is supposed to have fulfillment in him. He is affable, accessible, imposing in appearance, with a quiet dignity, gentlemanly, courteous, puts his case briefly and well and strictly to the point, says much in little, and is physically and mentally equipped for his office.

He stated the position of his church and its relations to the country, and what he regarded as persecutions and injustice, calmly and gently, without a hint of hate or passion, as if he were outside of it all and quite disinterested. There was no touch of resentment in tone, manner or look. He is of the highest order of teachers of a new faith. In perfect gentleness of speech and manner he resembles what the sacred books of the East tell us of the speech and manner of Buddha, "the blessed one." There are amiability and benevolence in his countenance, he gives and invites confidence, and I felt that I could say anything to him without fear of misconstruction. No portraits of him or of President Cannon, in books or magazines or illustrated papers, do either of them justice. Those of President Taylor make the face too hard, and denude it of all that is gentle and calm and handsome in it. Those of President Cannon give a twist of cunning to his features, which I could not find in his face.

I do not think that justice has been done by outsiders to the secular aspects of Mormonism. Due account has not been taken of

4

Great Salt Lake.

the social advancement which has come to the poor of all lands, who have come to Salt Lake to the church, and due credit for this has not been given to the church. A wall runs along in front of the Lion House, which was built for protection from thieves and Indians in the early days of the settlement. But for this wall intervening, the door of the President's room would open directly on the street. All the arrangements are of the utmost simplicity, and so as to make access easy. There are no barriers, nor anything nor anybody in the way of easy entrance and convenient exit.

The President's secretary kindly became our guide to Temple and Tabernacle for a closer inspection of these buildings. In the Tabernacle we stood at one end ; at the other end, in front of the organ, a gentleman dropped an ordinary-sized, common, small pin, and we heard it drop. He brushed his hand over the covering of the crimson-covered seats, and we heard that also. A whisper at one end can be heard at the other, and one or two of our party tested that likewise. These facts attest the perfect acoustic properties of the Tabernacle. We were taken to the office of the *Deseret Evening News*, the official organ of the church. We missed an interview with the editor, who was not in ; but we met the assistant editor, a man of impressive physique, and said to be a capable speaker and writer.

At 4:30 P. M. we leave Salt Lake City by the Utah Central Railway for Ogden, thirty-seven miles distant. Twenty miles away from the city we come alongside Salt Lake, forty by ninety miles in extent, and at an altitude of 4,218 feet. We run alongside of it for miles, having its flat, marshy-looking shores on one side, and the mountains on the other. Mormon settlements, flourishing and fair to see, abound, amid trees and fresh, pleasant surroundings.

Except from the mouth of a master of speech, or the pen of genius, how impotent are words to define these Western scenes. Such altitudes, such depths, an atmosphere so clear, so rarefied, such radiance of sunlight, night coming on in gorgeous sunsets, tinting the horizon with ever-varying masses of untranscribable colors. Then, when night has come, the moon floods the heavens with a loveliness, and the stars light it with a splendor, unobserved by me elsewhere. To these succeed the splendid surprise of morning, when the sun rises in his strength, and rides like a conqueror over summits white with age and snow.

We leave Ogden at 5:15 P. M., and early Wednesday morning are in San Francisco, 842 miles from Ogden. Monday night,

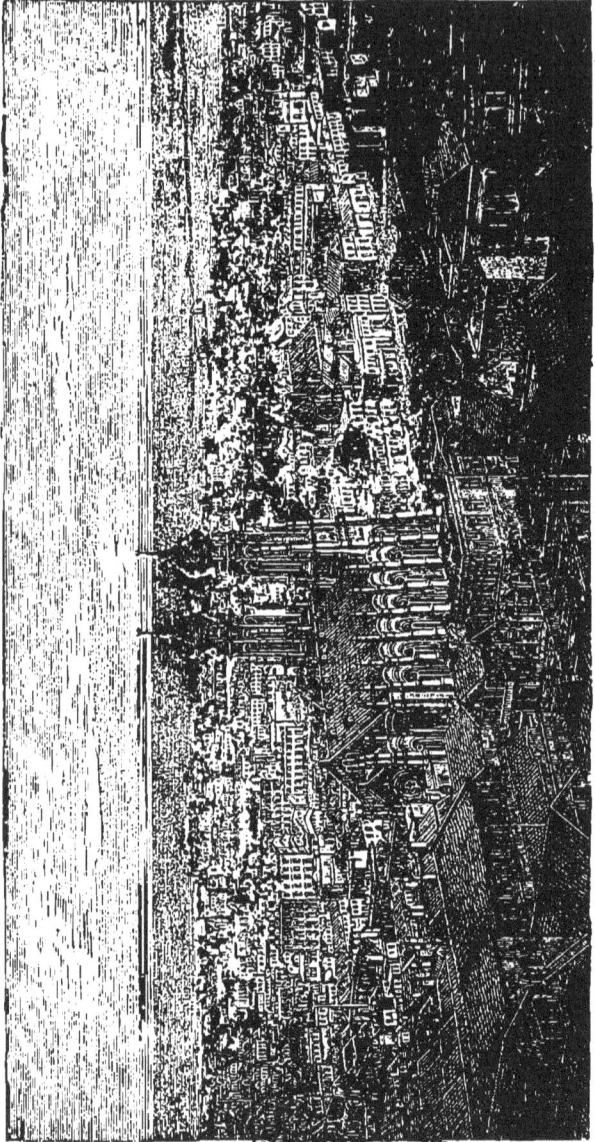

View of San Francisco

Tuesday and Tuesday night are occupied by this portion of our trip. Even after leaving Ogden, and while speeding on the journey over the Central Pacific Railway, we still have Salt Lake in sight for some distance. We pass a night camp of Chinese track-men, the offense of which to our nostrils was rank. We are on high table land, with mountains around us, many with much snow on them. Tuesday we are passing over the alkali plains. Wild sage is their chief product. The alkali dust, penetrating everywhere, and powdering us all over, is an unmitigated nuisance. Jack rabbits occasionally appear; Indians are seen riding on the platforms of express and baggage cars, and papooses strapped to their mothers' backs. Here and there this alkali plain and sage bush desert presents the charming surprise of little dots of luxuriant tropical vegetation, where at dining or other stations, it has been transformed by irrigation and cultivation. Then, there are fountains and flowers and the dense shade of trees, a delightful oasis in an otherwise barren land.

Tuesday night we pass the Sierras, and see them not. We also pass through thirty miles of snow-sheds, which we do not regret passing at night. In the early hours of the morning we are in Sacramento City, and see somewhat of the attractive Sacramento valley. Soon we are running by the inland waters of the Pacific, and now are at Oakland, cross by ferry to San Francisco, and take up our temporary abode at the Palace Hotel. On this trip I frequently heard the word "globe-trotters" applied to travelers who go long distances, or round the world. The inland waters of the Pacific, extending back from San Francisco, are extensive enough to entitle them to the distinction of being regarded as a separate ocean. The Palace Hotel is seven stories high, with accommodations for a formidable army. Carriages drive under cover right into the centre of the building in front of the hotel office. From the galleries of each story of this large quadrangle you can look down on the bustle and rush of numerous arrivals and departures. Elevators convey you from floor to floor, without your having to undergo the labor of climbing stairs.

It was night before we could find time to visit the Chinese quarter. There are 40,000 Chinese in San Francisco, most of whom are packed in one quarter. The sidewalks were crowded, and the interiors were literally packed. This quarter of the city is entirely given up to "the heathen," and we might just as well be in the Celestial Empire as here.

In this quarter we saw a building which was once the leading hotel in San Francisco. It is so no more. No hotel depending upon the patronage of the general public can exist in the Chinese quarter. The general public would not locate there even temporarily. Nothing that esteems itself white and good will dwell in this Nazareth. Chinese merchants can pack more merchandise and crowd more assistants in a given space than any white man can do. We explored one store, and were courteously received. Every available niche was filled up with merchandise, or had " a pagan " jammed in it, busy as a bee over books or correspondence. We visited a joss house, and were just becoming interested in the explanations and the marvels of engraving and carving which adorned it, when one of our party was overcome with the odor of the incense, and we beat an unceremonious retreat.

Our next visit was to a tea-garden. The charge for a cup of tea in a first-class tea-garden is just a trifle exorbitant ; but then, we were notified, the moment we ordered tea, what the charge would be. This is a refinement of fair play unusual outside of paganism. We quickly discovered that we had never tasted tea before. It is a celestial drink as made by " the heathen Chinee," and a much finer article of tea than is furnished to barbarians through the usual channels of trade. The Mongolian makes it in a way of his own, and the art of making tea still continues to be a monopoly of his.

We did not see the worst of this Chinese quarter. That, I am told, is indescribable. Opium dens abound, and smells are too pronounced for the most callous nostrils. If plague should come, the presence of this unsavory, closely packed crowd, would be a menace to public health. I was afterward taken through streets of low resort which my guide informed me were more dangerous than any in the Chinese quarter. These were occupied by French outcasts.

" Frisco," as the people of the far West delight to call the great city of the Pacific coast, is a city set upon several hills and in numerous valleys. It is well provided with large and elegant hotels, and beautiful and roomy street cars run everywhere. The street car lines are run by underground cable, the most practicable method where such heights have to be ascended. I have not seen as good street cars in any other city. Flowers grow like weeds in this " glorious climate."

Friday, August 8th. We left Frisco at 3:30 P. M., for Monterey, 125 miles distant. We pass Belmont and Menlo Park, the lovely Santa Clara valley, and its metropolis, San José, and fields in which the industrious " Chinee " is gathering up all the fat of the land.

HOTEL DEL MONTE — MONTEREY

At 7:25 p. m., we alight at a pretty little station in a land of flowers. The Hotel Del Monte is close at hand, "in a grove of 126 acres of oak, pine, spruce and cypress trees, and within a quarter of a mile of the beach." In the large hall of this great hotel, in a fireplace of generous dimensions, a log fire was blazing. The daintiest rooms daintily furnished look out on flower gardens which realize dreams of fairy land. Seven thousand acres of land are held in connection with this hotel, through which are twenty-five miles of carriage drives. We were told that we ought to see this and all California in winter, when flowers and everything else are finer than in summer. It is a paradise of flowers which bloom all the year round.

Saturday, August 9th, we took a drive of many miles, through the lovely grounds of the Hotel del Monte, and outside of them to the seashore, past a large bathing house, and through Monterey and Pacific Grove, a village of tents and seaside residences, a famous bathing resort "open all the year round," to Cypress Point. Surely and not very slowly goes on the progress of reclaiming the sandy wastes on the seaside of Hotel del Monte, and turning their barrenness into trees and flowers.

At Monterey we see the hotel at which Fremont took up his quarters after his trip across the continent, in 1846, which won for him the title of "the Pathfinder," and was the first step in fame which led to his being afterward nominated as the Republican candidate for president. With thought of Fremont comes his wife, the famous daughter of a famous father, Senator Benton, whose statue stands in La Fayette Park, St. Louis, who was one of the earliest, if not the earliest, advocates of a railroad across the continent to the Pacific. It was he who, in reference to this track across the continent, and pointing westward, said, "There is the East : there is India."

There is—

WHALING AT MONTEREY.

Monterey Argus, August 2.

The whalers shot a large female whale during the week ; but she sunk in about forty-five fathoms, and they will have to wait for her to come to the surface, which will take about three days. She is accompanied by her calf, which they expect to capture. Soon after shooting this one, they espied the male, and, giving chase, soon sent a bomb into his body. They were more successful in this instance; for the monster made for the bay, and towed the boats a considerable distance toward the place before he died. This one was more considerate than his mate; for he floated when life was extinct. He is a monster, measuring over eighty feet in length, and is known to the whalers as the "sulphur bottom." A large number of people from Monterey and Pacific

Grove visited the whalery Thursday, and sat on the beach watching the men remove the blubber. They expect to get seventy or eighty barrels from him. This is one of the largest whales ever caught in this section.

In Monterey we saw also the old Custom House, with its ancient flag-staff, on which the flag of the United States was first floated in California when the latter was ceded to the Union. We saw, too, the old fort and barracks, and the now somewhat wrecked looking building in which the collective wisdom of California once sat, for Monterey was once the capital of this State.

In 1849, when Bayard Taylor was here, it looked to him at first as "a deserted town." It has not quite lost that look yet. Then buildings " rented for $1,200 monthly," and rooms for $200 monthly, and " a lot 75 feet by 25 feet, with a small frame store upon it, was sold for $5,000. A one-story house, with a lot about 50 by 75 feet, in the outskirts of the town, was held at $6,000. This was about the average rate of property." Monterey has not fulfilled the hopes of its early days, when it was assumed to have advantages which San Francisco had not, and was expected, in some respects, to become a rival of San Francisco. It was to be one of the great cities, if not *the* great city, of the Pacific coast. It is now a fishing village and a pleasure resort, only that, and nothing more ; but it has the loveliest site in the world, and its climatic advantages are beyond question.

By the roadside, close to a point at which we crossed a small stream, there was a wooden cross inscribed " July 3, 1770." We are told that it marks the spot where the first service of the church was performed by the first Jesuit missionary. At Cypress Point, we take in a long sweep of Pacific shore. We look from the rocky height on the waters of the Pacific dashing about the rocks, and sprinkling Pelican Rock with its spray. Flocks of pelicans cover the rocks, and sail above the waters from rock to rock. Sea-lions popped up their heads, and made their presence known audibly. One looked inquiringly, and I think had it in his mind to ask us of his relatives which we had left behind us in Lincoln Park, Chicago, not far from our doorstep. It is from this coast the sea-lions are recruited for this Chicago park.

Our drive lay through pine forests and cypress groves of intense, pleasing and healthful odors. The high winds have flattened these cypresses, and bent and twisted and battered branches and leaves into one compact mass of fantastic forms. The shade is thick and perfect. California lilac and wild flowers met the eye every-

Cliff House and Seal Rocks, San Francisco.

where. Spanish moss lightly veiled trees. We had pointed out to us a creeping plant known as " Poison Oak," and were told fearful tales thereof. To some persons, to touch it is to absorb its poison. Very sensitive persons absorb the poison by merely passing near the plant. Our driver was skeptical as to this. He held that the wind must blow something of it against any passer-by in any case in which the latter caught the poisonous infection. " The fastest train on the Pacific coast" took us into San Francisco in time for a late dinner.

Sunday, August 10th. We went to the Cliff House, to look from its veranda on the rocky shores of the Pacific far below, and to see one of the great sights of San Francisco,—the crowds of sea-lions disporting in the water, and barking at nothing in particular. The waters were alive with them, and the rocks which were not preëmpted by sea-gulls were covered with them. They look their prettiest in the water, and their movements are swift and not ungraceful. They climb upon the rocks in the clumsiest way, and waddle down them and roll off them clumsily and ludicrously. When they lie on the rocks, as they do until they dry, they look to the eye as so many brown skins lying drying in a rather eccentric tannery.*

We diverged to a fine, large park, with drives and romantic pathways, and an endless array of flowers and bedding plants, and shrubbery and trees, and wild woods and greensward of the greenest, kept so by unwearied sprinkling. Frisco empties out its thousands on Sundays to Oakland, Alameda, Cliff House, etc. We crossed the bay by ferry to Oakland to visit friends. We went a few miles by rail, and then had a carriage drive of many miles through all that pleasant suburb and the fair land that lies all around it. Outside of Oakland's beautiful streets and splendid residences inclosed in lovely grounds, we were impressed with the fruit farms and the wealth and profusion of flowers. Eucalyptus trees of Australia, beautiful and

---

* The following is from a San Francisco dispatch of August 15th, in the Chicago *Tribune* of August 16th, 1885 : "The question of the destruction of food fish in the harbor by sea-lions has been discussed very often in connection with the diminution of the supply. An effort is now being made to secure all the evidence obtainable on this point. Fish Commissioner Redding has appointed a commission to take the testimony of experts. Should the report sustain the position of the fishermen, it is probable that the law forbidding the killing of sea-lions will be repealed. If this is done the Seal Rocks of the Cliff House, near the Golden Gate, one of the most famous resorts on the Pacific coast, where hundreds of seals and sea-lions daily bask in the sun, will soon be deprived of the only attractions for tourists."

tall and straight, abound. They are said to preclude malaria, and are cultivated as a protection to health. But nothing is safe from slander and detraction, not even this delight of the eye and defense against malaria, and I read in a newspaper:—

THE FALL OF AN IDOL.

The eucalyptus tree has hitherto been in favor for its anti-malarial properties, which are especially familiar in Australia, where it is one of the loftiest of timber trees. It has, however, lately lost favor in the province of San Pedro, Brazil, from the belief that it stimulates the generation of a poisonous dragon fly, which attacks all living creatures, to which its sting is fatal in a few minutes. The destruction of all eucalyptus trees has therefore been ordered in San Pedro.

San Pedro may have a demoralizing atmosphere, and evil communications may have there corrupted the good manners of the eucalyptus tree ; but, in the virtuous soil and " glorious climate of California," it retains its pristine qualities and the good opinion of the citizens, adorns the landscape, and remains a thing of beauty. Redwood is largely used in California for building. Of this species of " Mammoth California Trees," the Santa Clara, Cal., *Republican* says :

A redwood tree cut in this county furnished all the timber for the Baptist Church in Santa Rosa, one of the largest church edifices in the county. The interior of the building is finished in wood, there being no plastered walls. Sixty thousand shingles were made from the tree after enough was taken for the church. Another redwood tree, cut near Murphy's mill, in this county, about ten years ago, furnished shingles that required the constant labor of two industrious men for two years before the tree was used up.

It was incessantly dinned in our ears, that, to see California aright, we ought to see it in winter. Then there would be no fogs, the mountains would be green, and everything fresher and fairer. Even the flowers would be lovelier, and there would be other and finer varieties of them. At Monterey it was said, Come in winter if you wish to see Monterey when it is loveliest, and the whole land at its best. What a land, with an equable atmosphere and flowers all the year round.

As we first approached Frisco by rail, running alongside the inland waters of the Pacific Ocean, we had noticed grain in sacks piled in the open air, without any protection. At the extreme ends of long wharves running far out into the water, it was similarly piled. At that time of the year, there was no danger from rain, and none from winds coming to ruffle the vasty deep. It was a novelty to be in a land of such absolute certainty as to visitations of wind and rain.

Monday, August 11th. At 10 A. M., we take passage on the Queen of the Pacific, one of a line of steamers running between Frisco and Tacoma, at the head of Puget's Sound, via Victoria, Vancouver's Island, British Columbia. Our objective point was Portland, Oregon, and our original plan was to go direct by steamer running via Columbia river ; but we were told that it was rough crossing the bar at the mouth of the Columbia, and that the route via Victoria would take but a day longer, that the steamers were finer, that we would have more of the Pacific Ocean, and sights of greater interest, and we were persuaded.

We were told of the fine view of Frisco which we would have while sailing over the bay, and out of the Golden Gate into the great ocean beyond; but one of Frisco's solid fogs came down, and covered all the land, and bay, and sea, and our view was, consequently, an extremely limited one. We see the defenses being erected at the narrow passage known as the Golden Gate. The shores are soon hid by fog, and remain hid until 10 A. M., next day, Tuesday, August 12th. The fog blocks our view, and restricts it, to a few feet of water. At last it clears rapidly, like a veil lifted, and miles of sea sparkling in sunlight are revealed. The sun on the water is most dazzling. The shore comes out into sight. At starting, it was rocky; now it seems to be sand-hills, with higher hills behind. Birds of strong wing, pelicans and sea-gulls are following us. Numerous whales come in sight; but we miss them.

The first night we were advised to lie with our state-room door open. At half past 10, electric lights in state-rooms are extinguished. The watchman goes his steady rounds all night. Our state-room faces out to sea, and it is but one step from it to the side of the steamer. We lie with the Pacific Ocean at our sleeping-room door, and look out on it and its fogs, and listen to its dashings, which have a never-failing charm for me. Of the sound of ocean, like love for the beloved, you can not define the charm; but all the more exquisitely you feel it. The Pacific Ocean is not always as pacific as its name might imply. We listened to terrible stories about· its wrath from old voyagers who had made trips to and from China; and our experience was not all serene. Monday we had wind and fog; Tuesday morning, fog again, till suddenly it lifted, and the sun shone over miles of sparkling water. Then the ocean became as smooth as a village pond. Tuesday night we had wind and rain. Wednesday morning it was squally, but there was no sea to talk about.

Not many sail were seen. Monday and Tuesday we saw none;

Wednesday we saw a steamer and two sailing vessels. We kept on the lookout for whales, and on Wednesday, about 6 P. M., were rewarded by seeing them in any number, spouting and plunging in all directions, on all sides of us, near and far. Where sea and sky met, we saw a column of water spouting up to the heavens above, and immediately the huge figure of a whale was outlined on the horizon.

Much attention was paid to the comfort of passengers, more than I had ever experienced before. The captain came round daily about 11 A. M. to inspect and inquire if all was right, watchmen inspected every night after the electric light was extinguished, and waiter and stewardess were round between 6 and 7 A. M., with tea or coffee and toast, and to find out if we were going to breakfast. They came round after every meal to find out if we had been at it, and if we wished for anything.

Early Thursday morning, August 14th, we are in Victoria harbor, having accomplished our short sea voyage of about seven hundred and fifty miles. A. had telegraphed us before we left Frisco that he would come on from Portland, and meet us here. I was speedily on the dock, notwithstanding a mocking intimation that I need not expect him at that hour, and I surely could not expect that he would sit up all night waiting our arrival. Teamsters and cabbies in crowds assailed me; but I heeded not their cry, and kept steadily threading my way past them. Soon an open carriage came dashing swiftly down the steep road to the dock. It clearly had a mission, and I was sure that it was to me. I discerned a familiar figure, and soon a well-known voice said, "I am glad you have come."

Our steamer was to lie there until noon, and then go on its way to Tacoma; but A. decided that I had business to which to attend, people and sights to see, and must remain all day in Victoria, and go to bed at night in the steamer Olympian, of the Oregon Railway & Steam Navigation Company, which would leave early next morning for Tacoma, thus enabling me to make the whole trip from Victoria in daylight.

Vancouver's Island seemed to me the same as California, except in bustle and rush. Victoria seemed a city in Lotos Land. Nobody who was anybody got up early in the morning, and nobody was in a hurry. Even the newspapers appeared to be published for the name of the thing, and not for any news which they contained. They were as absolutely devoid of news, foreign or domestic, as perhaps it is permitted to a newspaper to be. There was nothing sensational about them except their price, which was ten cents a paper. That Victoria can digest its daily press and survive the operation speaks volumes for the healthiness of its climate. The deadness and dullness of the papers transcend description and baffle conception.

Vancouver is mountainous and beautiful, with rocky and wooded shores. We took a long inland, woodland, rural drive. Our drive included the Navy Yard, in which were English vessels of war, and took us past gardens and farms, with flowers and fruit, which seemed California over again. The Chinese excel in field culture here, as they do everywhere. We drove through the grounds, and past the residence of the Lieutenant Governor. In the grounds a convict gang were working on the carriage drive. Splendor and squalor, rank and crime, come into close contrast in all lands. We stopped at the Driard House, an unrivaled hotel. I do not think that it has its superior in table anywhere.

Victoria is the capital of British Columbia, which is one of the provinces of the Dominion of Canada. Like the province of Ontario, it has only one House of Parliament, and seems, like Ontario, to get along with one house just as well, and a great deal cheaper, if not a great deal better, than provinces and states that can not exist without a House of Representatives and a Senate. Why the people should elect a House of Commons and a Senate to check, and hold in rein, and delay, and embarrass, the House of Commons, is one of those mysteries which can only be solved by referring it to the wisdom of our ancestors.

The government buildings, six in number, are built of brick, are ornamental, pretty, and rather toyish in appearance. In the House of Representatives, which was not in session, there were twenty-five seats, one seat in excess of the number of members. On the edge of the government grounds, close to the highway, stands a granite shaft on a granite base, with this inscription :—

ERECTED BY THE PEOPLE OF
BRITISH COLUMBIA
TO THE MEMORY OF
SIR JAMES DOUGLAS, K. C. B.,
GOVERNOR
AND
COMMANDER IN CHIEF
FROM
1851 TO 1864.

What is fame? Outside of British Columbia, who has heard of this famous man in whose honor this stately column lifts its lofty head?

Victoria has a fine location, has 8,000 inhabitants, and, when Parliament is in session, must be a trifle livelier than when I walked its streets. On one street corner there was a sign with a famous name:—

GENERAL ASSORTMENT OF FANCY GOODS.	MRS. SHAKESPEARE.	BERLIN AND ZEPHYR WOOLS.

The next day I saw, in New Tacoma, a reminder of Dickens in the name of the "Weller House;" and later, in Portland, I had a reminder of Thackeray in the "Esmond House," at which I put up. I am sorry to say, that since then, this, the finest hotel in Portland, has been totally destroyed by fire.

The Canadian government had a commissioner in Victoria hearing evidence on the Chinese question. There are 18,000 Chinese in British Columbia, and 3,000 of these in Victoria. The commissioner elicited the fact that the low Chinese are very dirty and very bad, just as dirty and bad as low white people. The real crime of "the heathen" is not his vice and his dirt, in which he does not excel white outcasts, but that he works for less money, and can live upon less, than a white man. The real question to be determined is: Shall he, by his cheap labor, drive the white laborer to the wall? That is not the way the politicians state it, and that is not the cry raised by those who yell the loudest that the Chinese must go; but it is the exact position.

It is not a question of vice, or disease, or opium habits. It is a question of whether the cheap Mongolian shall replace the dear Caucasian. It is a question of race, and survival of the fittest and best, and must be met and dealt with in that way some day. This Chinese question is a burning one on the Pacific coast; but hitherto there seems to have been some hesitancy in dealing with it plainly and bluntly. Everywhere that the Chinaman is met, he confirms what Bayard Taylor wrote of him over thirty years ago, "He has the one virtue of industry, and his cheap habits of life enable him to get a profit out of bars deserted by the white miners, and soil scorned by the white farmers."

People engaged in the ordinary avocations of life go everywhere nowadays. Traveling is no longer the exclusive privilege of the rich or adventurous, or those having ample leisure. It is undertaken

for pleasure, for information, for business ; by the busy, the over-
worked, the most inadventurous. An excursion to Alaska had
passed a few days before my advent in Victoria. It left Portland,
Oregon, about the first of August ; and it was calculated that
the trip from Portland to Alaska and return, giving sufficient time for
sight-seeing, would take but twenty-one days. The fare was only $95.
About one hundred people took advantage of this excursion, seventy-
five of whom were school teachers spending their vacation. They
had been in attendance at the National Convention of Teachers held
in Madison, Wisconsin. After the convention adjourned, the
teachers scattered in all directions on pleasure trips before returning
to their homes.

I had looked upon Alaska as being almost inaccessible, and
waked up to find it an ordinary pleasure resort, to which you
can buy cheap round-trip tickets, just as you can buy them to
any other pleasure resort. This is one result of the building of the
Northern Pacific Railroad, and its being officered and operated by
wide-awake citizens, who omit no chance to open new avenues
of travel and develop new sources of traffic. Excursions to the
Yellowstone National Park and to Alaska are of their invention.

Some of these teachers, Alaska excursionists, on their return trip
overtook me at the Dalles, Oregon, and I found out from them that
our received ideas about Alaska stand in need of considerable
revision. They were so charmed with their trip that they laid plans
at once for another one in 1885.

Just before I left home I had a letter from Jerusalem, insisting
that I must go there ; and I was told by another friend to consider
myself under contract to visit the Yellowstone region within a
reasonable period. On my way west, I received a telegram
reminding me that I had agreed whenever called upon to make a
trip to Mexico. If that Alaska excursion had not gone, I should
have been strongly tempted to join it. When we first set out from
Chicago, we had about determined not to go west of Colorado,—at
any rate not to go beyond Salt Lake ; but, by taking advice
and yielding to persuasion, we found ourselves at last in Victoria,
the farthest point at which we touched.

Friday, August 15th. Last night we occupied state-rooms
on the steamer "Olympian," and, before going to bed, I had a moonlight view of the bay in which our steamer lay. I was up between
4 and 5 ; but, before I could get washed and dressed, the steamer
got under way, and so rapidly that we were out of the harbor before

5

I could get on deck. In about two hours we had steamed across the straits, which were calm and smooth as a pond, the beautifully wooded shores of Vancouver were receding from view, and we were in Puget's Sound, "the Mediterranean of the Northwest." The snowy head of lofty Mount Baker was just visible through a rift in fleecy clouds.

Our first stop was at Port Townsend, Washington Territory, a fine location, with business houses and hotels on the shore close to the water, and residences on the highlands, which rise steep and abrupt from the narrow strip of land at their feet between them and this inland sea. From the mouth to the head of the sound at Tacoma, W. T., is about one hundred and fifty miles. There was everywhere ample breadth, which sometimes counted by miles. It was novel to me to find myself on this great inland salt-water sea, hemmed in by lofty and beautifully wooded mountains and highlands; and I remained on deck all day except during dinner, enjoying the varied scenes which presented themselves in one long and enchanting panorama. The reflected rays of the sun had given my face the dark red tint of the Indian before I reached Tacoma. Dinner was considerately served in a saloon, the windows of which commanded both sides of our course, and the way by which we had come, so that no sight-seeing was lost to us. Of constant recurrence were immense outlets on each side of us, stretching away we knew not how far, and as broad or broader than that in which we were plowing our way.

Of picturesque places on the sound, where all were picturesque, Seattle, W. T., was the most prominent; rising from the water, extending right back on the hills, showing to the utmost advantage its charming residences, and fine business blocks, and public buildings, and, most to its credit, largest and most striking, its public schools and university buildings, splendid and imposing. Nothing in the place was quite as good as these halls of learning, and it is needless to say that Seattle commanded at once unhesitating respect.

We had two or three hours of daylight left when we reached New Tacoma, W. T., at the head of navigation and the sound. We took rooms at "The Tacoma," an imposing palatial structure, splendidly furnished, and in grounds tastefully laid out. It stands, as nearly all New Tacoma stands, high above the sound; and the best views of the city and surrounding country can be obtained from it. Beyond all comparison, it is the largest and best building in the place, and is one of the most comfortable hotels in the country. It was built and is maintained to popularize New Tacoma, and was not expected to pay; but it does pay. New Tacoma is perhaps the foremost city on the sound. Old Tacoma is over the hills, in another bay. But the two places are gradually nearing each other, and have been incorporated as one city.

As we drove over to Old Tacoma, Saturday, August 16th, we found workmen cutting away and burning the forest, and improving the communications by road, leveling and straightening it out. The road stood in need of widening. There was no room to pass, except at special points ; and we had to stop till a team got out of our way, and sometimes we had to keep others waiting in the same way for us. These passing points were utilized by teamsters for purposes of gossip, and we were kept waiting at one point till two who were ahead of us had exchanged news with each other and departed on their separate ways. There is a large waste of timber going on in this country, where much is burnt merely to get it out of the way.

The most noticeable thing in Old Tacoma was the bell tower of the Episcopal Church. It is simply a tree with the top sawn off even, and the bell fixed thereon. The Episcopal Church is a shanty adorned with a cross. The æsthetic fever has reached New Tacoma, and we saw several "dude" houses, pleasantly diversifying the ordinary sameness of city architecture. Mr. C. B. Wright, of Philadelphia, has given $50,000 as an endowment fund to the Annie Wright Seminary for Young Ladies, a large three-story building which he has erected in New Tacoma. Next to "The Tacoma," this seminary is the best building in the place. It is named after a daughter of Mr. Wright. He has also erected, at his own expense, an Episcopal church, which has cost him $25,000 ; and he has projected an educational institution for young men, which he will endow with $50,000. He is, I believe, interested in "The Tacoma," and other city property, as well as in the railways here, and is fully discharging, with lavish hand, all the duties which property owes to a community.

New Tacoma is well provided with schools. An election was in progress while I was there. In the Third Ward four names of ladies headed four gentlemen on the nomination ticket. This was probably reversed when election day came. Extensive fires had swept away blocks, and much building was going on. Iron foundries, at an expense of $2,000,000, are to be established, and to give employment to 2,000 people.

The veranda of " The Tacoma " looks down upon the head-waters of the inland sea-waters, which here lose themselves in shallow grass and marsh. I sat for an hour or more looking down upon this farthest advance inland of these Pacific floods, and at the opposite shore, wooded and hilly ; at the Indian mission and school in the distance ; at Mount Tacoma, formerly Mount Rainier, about sixty-seven miles away, 14,300 feet high, forty miles in circumference at its base, and with a superficial area of 1,600 miles. Thick clouds wrapped all of it except its head and base, and there was more snow upon it than on any mountain which I have seen. In the intervening woods, near the city, lies an enchanted land of drives and lakelets.

While I sat, a young bear belonging to the hotel grounds began to climb the veranda steps, possibly with the intention of opening social relations with me. He was not a bear of determined character, but was rather hesitating. He deliberated at every step, debating every move. About half way up he took a vote and decided to return. At the foot he reconsidered the motion, turned his face upward, raised his paws on the first step, took them down again to think it over another time, pondered profoundly and heavily, scratched his head and clawed out an idea, and turned and departed. Afterward he came again a few times, but could never make up his mind what course to take : he was a bear of a very undecided turn of mind. I did not care for his company anyway.

Mr. Ackley, formerly of North Shields, now employed on a city paper here, called, and introduced himself as a Northumbrian. I had a most pleasant interview with him. He knew many known to me in Newcastle-upon-Tyne and the North of England.

New Tacoma has a Chinese quarter with a population of about five hundred.

Saturday, August 16th, at 6 P. M., we leave Tacoma by train. We go 105 miles by rail, and at 11 P. M., at Kalama, we take the steamer, and do the remaining thirty-eight miles by river. We are in Portland early next morning, Sunday, August 17th.

Portland has a population of 40,000, of which 10,000 are Chinese; it has "go" enough in it for a city of twice its population. Its traffic by rail and river is very large. East Portland, on the opposite side of the Willamette, is a considerable place. Twelve miles onward is the junction of the Willamette and Columbia rivers, the latter being the "Oregon" of old writers. Seventy years ago Bryant wrote,—

Portland and Mt. Hood.

"Take the wings
Of morning, traverse Barca's desert sands,
Or lose thyself in the continuous woods
Where rolls the Oregon, and hears no sound
Save his own dashings."

These lines are the perfect expression of complete solitude, and they have always invested the Oregon to me with all the hues of romance. They clung to my memory, and would not let me forget them, nor the mighty stream they celebrated, and there came a haunting wish to see it. Since the poet wrote, change has come to the Columbia, and fleets sweep over it, and trains rush along its shores, which are lined with farms and villages and salmon canneries, and at its mouth Astoria stands sentry.

Monday, August 18th, I devote to business and other visits, and drives in Portland, its parks and suburbs. Splendid, substantial, solid business blocks and beautiful residences abound. For a city of its size it has an amazing number of fine private residences. There was one fine street, palatial and pleasing. There live the pioneers, all in a row. They "came here in the forties," said my informant, and they sat still and grew rich because they couldn't help it. They had the land, and in the heart of this city it became valuable.

The drive to the City Park was like the ascents on the Denver & Rio Grande Railroad; we went up and up, and round and round, track above track, until we attained the highest point in the park, from whence we looked down upon Portland and wide spaces of landscape. Up a glorious ravine, and by roads like the road to the park, we drove out to the beautiful residence and grounds of hospitable Mr. Schultze, the Land Commissioner of the Northern Pacific Railroad. Forest fires away in the distance obscured the land, and prevented us from seeing all that we had been led to expect to see from this eminence. Mount Hood, the lion of the land, was not visible. It was the only famous mountain on our whole trip which declined to be at home to us.

In the city we passed what had once been a barren, stony ravine; but the industrious Chinaman has transformed it into a fruitful garden. At night we went to the Chinese theatre. The streets around it swarmed with Chinese; they were like ants on an ant hill. The theatre was crammed to suffocation; there was not even standing room left. A box had been reserved for us. The boxes next to us were filled with Chinese women of the only class, with rare exceptions, imported into this country. They were as quiet and undemonstrative as if they had not been outcasts. The audience were all very quiet,—almost stolid. They enjoyed themselves seriously ; scarcely a smile illuminated a countenance. There was more stir over something unknown to me which occurred in the audience than over anything going forward on the stage. There was a good deal of smoking, and fruits and candies were trafficked round.

The seats and boxes were of common wood, and a very few strips of Chinese patterns, and a few Chinese inscriptions, were the sum total of any decorations. The stage was an open platform, at each end of which there was a packed audience, through which the actors had to force their way out. There were three or four seats, and no more stage scenery than would furnish forth a Punch and Judy show. An indescribable orchestra sat at the rear of the stage, eternally assisting, and emphasizing points most noisily. Stage clears: orchestra clatters and deafens. Actors enter: orchestra clatters and deafens. Actors enter and make their exit at curtained entrances at the back of the stage on each side of the orchestra. They came in at the right of the orchestra, and made their exit at the left of the orchestra. I was told that an actor having to feign death lies awhile on the stage, and then gets up and walks out.

The only scenery I saw used was something like a pulpit, but not as large. Slight changes were made in it, and the actors also made slight changes on the platform during the action of the play. Except the few chairs, however, not much use was made of scenery, if that which was used can be dignified by that name. There were a few gorgeous costumes ; masks also were used, and fiends were made as uncanny as paper and paint could make them.

No females perform on the Chinese stage, and horrid males painted an inch thick took the female parts. The singing consisted of a poor, rasping chant, screeching, screaming and howling, and had less of music in it than ordinary speech. There was a circular hole at the back of the stage, high above the orchestra, and that appeared to be utilized by spectators. Chinese plays last for days and weeks. We contented ourselves with a small section of one. When we came outside late the streets were still jammed with heathen. I do not know how long the theatre remains open,— perhaps it never closes,—nor when the heathen sleep,—perhaps they keep awake always. They swarm on the streets at all hours.

Next day, Tuesday, August 19th, after business, I visited art galleries and studios, and saw marvelous effects in color, and wonderful

Palisades of Columbia River.

transcripts of wonderful scenery. Colonel Tom Merry, of the Portland *Oregonian*, did me the service to explain these monster mountain scenes and river scenes, which he did with clearness and facility, having lived among them, camped beside them, and faced them for months at a time. Mr. Stuart, whose studio I visited, had his right arm in a sling. He got it broken, having slipped on a glacier on one of the mountains a distance of 200 yards before he recovered himself.

Wednesday, August 20th, at 7 A. M., we leave on a steamer for The Dalles. This is the commencement of a continuous journey from Portland to St. Paul, 1,912 miles, which is to last up to the afternoon of Sunday, August 24th. We might have gone by rail from Portland; but we preferred the steamer trip of one day on the Willamette and Columbia rivers. At The Dalles we had time for supper before the train, which left at 11:40 A. M., overtook us. We had engaged sleeping berths on the train, and, when it overtook us, we had nothing to do but to step on board and take our assigned places. The Willamette looked spacious enough to fill the full measure of the description of the Columbia. The conjunction of the two rivers deserved the title of a lake.

The Columbia, what we saw of it on this day's trip, was simply an immense cañon filled by a correspondingly immense river. Fog and forest fires limited our sight-seeing ; mountains make our shores. Among the marvels of the rocky shores were Rooster Rock, Castle Rock, grotesque figures like sentries; palisades of varied kinds, high and low; at some points a perfect wall slanting away from the water, producing fine effects with the aid of sun and mist, or sunset; Multnomah Falls, and cascades like Niagara river above Niagara Falls. Curious rocks popped up here and there in this wonderful stream. Evidently these once had been one ; but the water had washed them apart. Rocky cones were numerous. The water had cut its way through the rocks. This was especially the case east of The Dalles, where the river dashed through many curious rocky channels which it had cut for itself.

The trip from Portland to The Dalles was made by steamer to the Cascades; then we took a train for a few miles past the Cascades; and then took another steamer for The Dalles, from whence we made the remainder of our trip to St. Paul by train. We passed large canneries, where salmon are canned, and saw the simple method of catching salmon wholesale.

After leaving The Dalles, and just before nightfall, we passed an Indian village, or encampment, close to the river. An Indian girl

Multnomah Falls, Columbia River.

was picking her way along the shore; an Indian man and boy, mounted on one horse, jogged indolently along; an Indian woman was rowing in a boat, and her "noble," melancholy red man sat at his ease therein. One Indian hut stood close to the river's edge, convenient for fishing, and subject to prompt change of base if the river should rise; and rivers out here are troubled that way. Some of the beds were outside of all shelter, with only the sky for a canopy. Indians of all ages and sexes were sprawling in all directions and attitudes, none of the latter graceful or picturesque, and some not quite decent. Old female Indians were withered, shriveled and ugly. Dirt and squalor! The noble red man? Oh, no! The dirty, lazy, thieving red man, devoid of all romance or grace, yet not quite devoid of interest, because he continues to be considerable of a nuisance and obstruction.

It were too long to tell of rivers, lakes and mountains with which we made acquaintance; of immense gorges through which we and the rivers ran, rivers which we cross and recross, and lose and find again endlessly. From our inner consciousness we evolve how a town is made. It is done by cutting down a few trees, and burning a few more, thus clearing a space in the woods sufficient for a few tents and wooden houses, then shooting somebody to start a cemetery, and the thing is done.

In one new town we saw an hotel. It bore the sign of "Palace Hotel," and promised fresh bread and beds. It was a long, wooden shanty of one room, with a "wash-room" at one side of it. Inferentially we came to the conclusion, that, after supper is served every evening, and the tables cleared, beds are then made up on the tables; and any high-toned, gilt-edged, kid-gloved guest, who is very particular and exclusive, can have a table to himself on payment of extra charge. Indians and Chinese abound on this route; the latter were imported to build the railroad, and remained to prey. We passed a graveyard with memorials erected by vigilants to those whom they had rooted out. It was but yesterday, so to speak, and that state of society has passed away so quickly that it will be myth to-morrow. Change comes so fast in new lands.

We passed a mountain on fire; it was more a blaze of weeds and grass than trees. The crossing of lake Pend d'Oreille on the railway was fine, and the scenery on the whole route was marvelous. It is well named "Wonderland" in books which treat of it.

Night and darkness reigned when we crossed the Missouri; but we got out on the rear platform of the car to strain our eyes to pierce

Lake Pend d'Oreille.

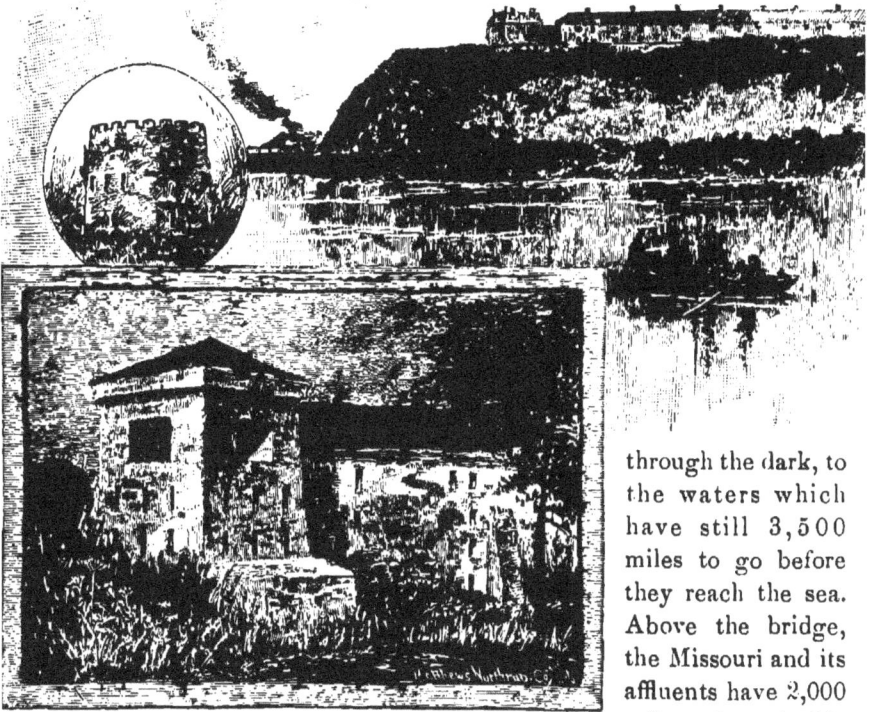

Fort Snelling.

through the dark, to the waters which have still 3,500 miles to go before they reach the sea. Above the bridge, the Missouri and its affluents have 2,000 miles of navigable waters.

We passed across Dakota at night, and missed its prolific wheat fields. It is estimated that Minnesota has 10,000 lakes, varying from one to thirty miles in diameter; we saw a fair percentage of them, and never tired of their infinite variety.

From Sunday, August 24th, to Tuesday, August 26th, we remained in St. Paul, with the exception of a carriage drive to Fort Snelling and the Falls of Minnehaha. Wednesday morning we were in Chicago, after our thirty-four days' travel of 6,610 miles, and after having seen some portion of one British province and thirteen States and Territories of the United States, not including Illinois, the State from which we started, and to which we returned.

www.ingramcontent.com/pod-product-compliance
Lightning Source LLC
Chambersburg PA
CBHW020336090426
42735CB00009B/1558